D0977173

Roots of Style

WEAVING TOGETHER
LIFE, LOVE, AND FASHION

A CELEBRA BOOK

CELEBRA
Published by New American Library, a division of
Penguin Group (USA) Inc., 375 Hudson Street,
New York, New York 10014, USA
Penguin Group (Canada), 90 Eglinton Avenue East, Suite 700, Toronto,
Ontario M4P 2Y3, Canada (a division of Pearson Penguin Canada Inc.)
Penguin Books Ltd., 80 Strand, London WC2R 0RL, England
Penguin Ireland, 25 St. Stephen's Green, Dublin 2,
Ireland (a division of Penguin Books Ltd.)
Penguin Group (Australia), 250 Camberwell Road, Camberwell, Victoria 3124,
Australia (a division of Pearson Australia Group Pty. Ltd.)
Penguin Books India Pvt. Ltd., 11 Community Centre, Panchsheel Park,
New Delhi - 110 017, India
Penguin Group (NZ), 67 Apollo Drive, Rosedale, Auckland 0632,
New Zealand (a division of Pearson New Zealand Ltd.)
Penguin Books (South Africa) (Pty.) Ltd., 24 Sturdee Avenue,
Rosebank, Johannesburg 2196, South Africa

Penguin Books Ltd., Registered Offices:
80 Strand, London WC2R 0RL, England

Published by Celebra, an imprint of New American Library,
a division of Penguin Group (USA) Inc.

First Printing, February 2012
10 9 8 7 6 5 4 3 2 1

LIBRARY OF CONGRESS CATALOGING-IN-PUBLICATION DATA:
Toledo, Isabel, 1961–
The roots of style: weaving together life, love and fashion / by Isabel Toledo ; illustrations by
Ruben Toledo
p. cm.
ISBN 978-0-451-23017-1
1. Toledo, Isabel, 1961– 2. Fashion designers—United States—Biography.
3. Women fashion designers—United States—Biography. 4. Fashion design—United States—History.
I. Title.
TT505.T62A3 2012
746.9'2092—dc23   2011043642
[B]

Set in Granjon
Designed by Pauline Neuwirth

Printed in the United States of America

PUBLISHER'S NOTE
While the author has made every effort to provide accurate telephone numbers and Internet
addresses at the time of publication, neither the publisher nor the author assumes any
responsibility for errors, or for changes that occur after publication. Further, publisher does not
have any control over and does not assume any responsibility for author or third-party Web sites
or their content.

To my father for his wisdom of style.

To my mother for the love of fashion.

To my sisters for providing me with their closets to raid.

To my second father, Pops Toledo, for exposing me to the professional landscape of fashion and to my mother-in-law, Oneida, for making Ruben.

Roots of Style

Introduction

WRITING THE INTRODUCTION

to this book is like opening the door to a

party, knowing that the room beyond is

filled with very well-dressed people and

I am totally naked. Dressing a woman is

something that I know very well how to

do. Dressing a book, on the other hand, takes a part of me that I have never explored. It is a vulnerable and intimate undertaking, not unlike the process of making clothes.

In fashion and in style, many truths are revealed. Style is common property; it belongs to all. Because it is constantly changing, fashion can be seen as something frivolous and superfluous. Both style and fashion elicit a wide range of emotions and can be infectious, even enthralling, provoking excitement in some people, revolution in others, and a heck of a lot of anxiety in a whole lot more. For me, style and fashion inspire optimism above all, while giving me the tools to communicate. Fashion is what time looks like, and that's something I take very seriously. Indeed, it is the very texture and weave of life. When First Lady Michelle Obama wore my coat and dress on that gloriously frozen Inauguration Day, I was woven into time, and into history itself. For me, a political refugee, that moment was an enormous accomplishment and a humbling gift from the universe.

Without fashion, I never would have had a voice. Now, with this book, I have examined the shape of my life from the inside as a way of connecting the dots between my own childhood as a girl growing up in Cuba and my life today as an independent fashion designer.

I consider this book a different kind of dialogue, a new way to share my views on life, love, and fashion design. The experience of writing it has been a bit like turning one of my own designs inside out to discover the backbone and study the central core of its construction. Through dissecting my personal style compass, the map of my life has emerged.

I was born into change, as my large and loving family was swept away by a sea of political and cultural upheaval after the Cuban Revolution and landed in the United States. Coming to America, I learned to merge my Caribbean soul with the ultra-slick cosmopolitan tempo of New York City. Change can provoke an inspired reshuffling of your deck of cards. It is circulation, movement, and a certain freedom of mobility. It is an opportunity for reinvention.

As an immigrant, I am privileged to observe and experience the wonder of living in America, and because of that, I certainly never take it for granted. The ability to plant your creative seed, grow, and prosper is the key to our culture's evolution. Our country may not be perfect and oftentimes living in the U.S. can sometimes be complicated and inconvenient, but it's certainly well worth the effort. Creatively, for me, it is the most fertile and stimulating climate on the planet. Our American population is made up of different ethnic, racial and religious backgrounds all living in such a wide range of terrains. The diversity of lifestyles and all the various economic classes that can participate in fashion contribute to fashion's richness.

All this great delicious mix is what makes this country so modern and so interconnected and able to pioneer the future. This clash of intentions and difference in purpose is freedom for the soul, and the main ingredient for my creativity.

My personal circumstances, brought on by political change, allowed me to define and discover myself, as I cultivated natural talents and curiosities. Through my love of make and the ability to follow my instincts, I was able to develop my passion for fashion design into a lifelong career.

Love fuels every aspect of my life and is woven into everything I do. Love was the guiding light that introduced me at a young age to my husband, the artist and illustrator Ruben Toledo, who fell in love at first sight with a shy dreamer of a girl.

I fell in love with Ruben's art first. It took
another four years for me to reciprocate and
realize that this kid was the love of my life. While
I was busy playing, sewing, dancing, and growing
up, I discovered that Ruben was the missing link, in
the best possible sense of those words. Love is often
the missing link in life. Once that element flowers, the
rest of life seems to flow along.

My time at the Met was instrumental because it was there
that I first understood the enormous impact that fashion has
on culture, and grasped the value of fashion as art. These
realizations led me to design new fashions and encourage
women to reveal their personalities through their inner fashion
IQs. We designers propose new ideas in every collection, some
of which are too early or too experimental. In the end, our
customers provide the ultimate collaborations, deciding what
will become fashion through their choices.
Fashion design moves forward when
people think for themselves and
dress their own minds and moods.

What makes fashion design so
fascinating for me is the combination
of opposite elements. Great designs
represent the logical, timeless, well

engineered, and well constructed. At the same time, fashion is the flavor of the day, the ephemeral, the feeling of the moment, the essence of something as intangible as air and atmosphere. These contradictory impulses are what make fashion so compelling. Fashion is as unpredictable as humanity itself. It is certainly a capricious journey of the human imagination. And we all participate in fashion, whether we sew it, champion it, pretend to ignore it, or detest it. Fashion may be the most democratic of all the art forms because we all have to go through the ritual of dressing ourselves every day.

Every time I create a new collection, I am weaving together the threads of my history, my experiences, and my emotions into cloth, texture, color, and shapes based on a woman's anatomy. I take into account body language, movement, a million practical things, and some technical breakthroughs. These are all hidden in the seams; a client never sees them if I do my job correctly. But she senses, I hope, the pleasure, delight, and balanced feeling you get when how you appear on the outside is in tune with how you feel—or want to feel—on the inside.

By showing my first collection in 1985, Ruben and I accidentally entered ourselves into the thrilling roller-coaster ride of the fashion business, with all of its hair-raising ups and downs. Fashion has taken us to many parts of the world, and my work soon became the subject of more than a few design exhibitions and has entered into some of the world's most prestigious historic costume collections.

By reading this book, I hope that you will find personal credos and observations that you can apply to your own life. Whether you are a fan of fashion, an aspiring artist or designer, or find pleasure in making things in your own home, I hope that these words will help you weave your own personal story into your style, as you discover your signature.

Part **1** life ......

1 *Discovering Roots*

I keep the valuable lessons I learned during my

early childhood years close to my heart. They

were the easiest to learn and the hardest to erase.

MY CHILDHOOD ROOTS HAVE

always been a true compass in both my

professional and personal life. Perhaps

because my parents made the painful decision

to leave Cuba after the Revolution in 1968, I

still carry precious, powerful memories of the

place and the people I loved there, and I

keep the valuable lessons I learned during

those early years close to my heart. They

were the easiest to learn and the hardest

to erase.

There is no such thing as a map or a safety net when you are an artist. But I have always used these childhood memories and lessons as touchstones whenever I need to tap into my emotions or question my next step as I create something new. Our childhood experiences help inform who we are, because it is then that we begin to discover our passions, talents, and habits. How I make clothes today is about how I think and feel, which in turn reflects how and where I grew up.

As a child in Cuba, I observed the interplay of light and shadow in Spanish Colonial architecture, absorbed the distinctive personal styles of my parents, learned about the importance of dressing emotions, and realized the power of womanhood in all its diversity. Taken together with the impact of coming to America, my earliest experiences gave me the foundation I needed to become a successful fashion designer.

I WAS BORN IN A place with beautiful rivers, sharp light and sleepy streets: Camajuani, Las Villas, Cuba, a small town located in the heart of the island among tobacco and sugarcane fields. Located about a three-hour drive from Havana, Camajuani is a tiny place with big dreams and even bigger people, a town famous for its yearly carnivals with fantastic floats, fireworks, and parrandas. I am the youngest of three children. Together with my sisters Any and Mary, we were known around town as Las Hijas de Izquierdo (The Daughters of Felix Izquierdo).

The way the light of the Caribbean sun hits this small corner of the universe magnifies all of the silhouettes. It was here that I first learned to see light and understand space. One of my strongest, most influential memories of Cuba is how the light shone so differently there from anywhere else I've ever been. I learned that sense of perception—the way we experience textures and colors—is subjective to the physical environment and space we live in. What seems right in the warm summer light can look harsh in the winter. Colors or textures that feel great in the misty gray of fall climates look downright depressing and dowdy in spring. This is the beauty of the seasons and the wonder of travel even within your own backyard where you have the possibility of resetting your eye and refocusing your perspective.

Our town was very Spanish with Colonial architecture. Our house, like many others in our town, was white stucco with a severe exterior. It had an interior that bloomed with brilliant colors in the patterns of the hand-painted ceramic tiles laid on the wall borders and floors. The repetitive patterns were mesmerizing and served as my gateway to meditation and contemplation.

The architecture all around me was made even more interesting by the soft geometric shapes formed by ornate ironwork on the verandas, stair railings, and window grilles. As a child, I remember sometimes feeling nearly blinded by the sun whitewashing a house, but still trying to peer into the depths of the deep green shade, or tracing the lacy shadows cast by the ironwork with my eyes. In this way, I became aware early on of the pleasing beauty of shapes, function, movement, and the subtle tones bleeding between contrasting colors. Here is where I learned to see light, feel contrasts, and understand space—three very important components of my work in fashion today.

Our house belonged to my grandmother, my father's mother. She was Spanish, and had been brought from the Canary Islands to Cuba by her sisters, who were already married and living on the island. This was an arranged marriage, in that my aunts brought their sister to marry my grandfather, a veteran of *La Guerra Chiquita*, and to be a mother to his seven children after his first wife died.

It was an elegant house. My grandmother had two sets of very formal living room furniture, beautifully crafted out of dark wood and cane. It was smooth and cool to the touch. What entranced me more, however, was the romantic shape of her sewing machine. This wasn't because my grandmother sewed her own clothes—I never saw her sit at the machine—it was because this machine seemed so mysterious an object.

The sewing machine had belonged to my grandfather's first wife. Because of this, it was kept in a place of honor and always remarkably polished, like an object in a museum. It looked like a sculpture, with its beautiful silver metal parts and intricate black iron body, only it was even better because it was a machine with parts that moved. I was the sort of child who loved machines because I was fascinated by how things worked; I took everything from dolls to bicycles apart to see how they were made.

I spent hours playing with my grandmother's sewing machine. I was a shy, quiet child, and I'd play in that magical space beneath it, in the cool quiet dark away from the household clamor created by my sisters, my parents, my grandmother, and the endless stream of relatives and friends who visited. I explored and moved each of that sewing machine's belts, pulleys, cogs, and circular spinning parts, sometimes pretending it was a magical vehicle, and always wondering what that machine could do.

Sewing machines still hold the same kind of magic and wonder for me. Learning how to use my babysitter's sewing machine just a few years later would help me start to find my voice and express my individuality. After that, there was no stopping me: Sewing became my way of sharing my most personal thoughts, feelings, and creative ideas with the world.

STYLE VS. FASHION

I'm often asked questions about style: Where does it come from? Is it hereditary? Can some cultures claim it more than others? Can style be learned, taught, made into a list and memorized, or put in a book of ingredients like recipes for a cookbook? I believe that style is common property. It belongs to no one, and to everyone.

I learned early on about the important distinction between style and fashion from both of my parents. My mother truly loved fashion, unlike my father, who had style.

My parents were both very direct, "tell it to me straight" people who were filled with practical wisdom and an amazing love of life. They taught me by example that I have to be who I am, even if it means sometimes being misunderstood. From them, I learned the value of being sincere in my expression, whether through my actions, my words, or the way I dressed. Being sincere meant showing the utmost respect and consideration for others. This lesson on the importance of sincere expression provided me with a 360-degree compass, and would later serve as the basis from which I approach style.

My father, Felix Izquierdo, was a great example of this. He went to work in our town's small hardware store when he was only twelve years old, and eventually became part owner. He had a great innate sense of timeless style. He would visit the

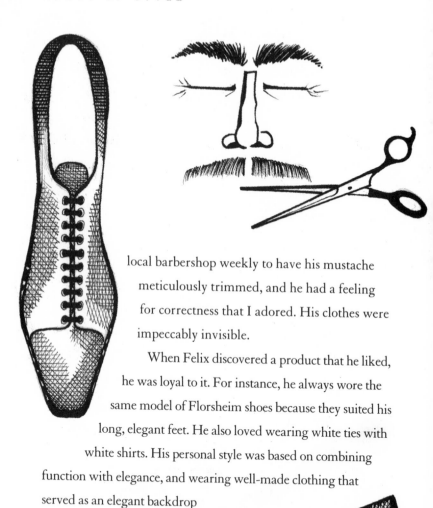

local barbershop weekly to have his mustache
meticulously trimmed, and he had a feeling
for correctness that I adored. His clothes were
impeccably invisible.

When Felix discovered a product that he liked,
he was loyal to it. For instance, he always wore the
same model of Florsheim shoes because they suited his
long, elegant feet. He also loved wearing white ties with
white shirts. His personal style was based on combining
function with elegance, and wearing well-made clothing that
served as an elegant backdrop
for his approachable
smile.

My mother, Bertha Perez, introduced me to the allure of fashion. She was romantic, attractive, and fiercely independent. She was the catcher for the neighborhood girls' baseball team, and worked outside the home with my father at the hardware store long before it was customary for women to work especially after their children were born.

"Birdy," as Ruben fondly called her, had a real flair for fashion. She was the opposite of my father, in that she didn't find one classic fashion that suited her free-spirited ways. Instead, her style was always about refreshing her wardrobe. She loved the novelty that fashion offered. Mother was always aware of the latest trends and would insist on trying them out on my poor older sisters. Florals, plaids, checks, and embroidered garments constantly rotated through her wardrobe, as she was always eager to try any new innovation that had a modern, international flavor.

Birdy loved saying, "I was born in a shoe box," because as a young woman, she had worked in her uncle's shoe workshop before marrying my father. She took pride in telling me how she would cut out images of shoes from magazines and have her uncle make them to her liking. She could tell where a shoe was made just by looking at it and touching it, whether that shoe was from Spain, Italy, the U.S., or anywhere else in the world. One of her favorite duties at the store was to choose the appropriate leather for the shoemakers in town. You see, Birdy was a leather connoisseur.

Not surprisingly, Mother always wore great leather shoes in unusual colors, like hunter green pumps, pearl gray sling backs, or Gothic-looking strappy sandals, and always with handbags to match. Ruben still remarks on how Birdy taught him how important shoes are in helping people form certain impressions of you. She was also fond of gold bracelets and cuffs, always wore a watch to keep her on time, and had her dresses perfectly tailored to fit.

What is the difference between fashion and style? Fashion is ephemeral. It is the flavor of the day, and useful for refueling your style inspiration when you feel you've run out of gas. Fashion is easy to apply because it's all surface.

Style, on the other hand, is an effective way to carve out your individuality. Style is content. A person with true style is displaying a fertile and thinking mind. The truth is, we're all born with an inner voice that serves as our personal style guiding light. To find it, we just need to tap into our instincts. When you are in touch with your inner self, your outer self projects balance and confidence. This is fertile ground for rooting style. The trick is that you have to learn to weave your own experiences together to arrive at your personal vision.

We are all born with a history, a style DNA. If you're happy with yours, build on it. Use it as your jumping-off point. Or, if you have outgrown your style, feel free to extrapolate and reinvent. That, after all, is what fashion is for. People with style dress in harmony with their inner, most authentic selves. The allure of personal style is to be in accordance with yourself first, and, by natural extension, with the world. Style is eternal.

Whereas style requires an inner participation and is self-motivated, fashion is all surface. Style blossomed before fashion arrived on the scene. Fashion set its goals on differentiating itself from the national costume and the regional customs. Fashion introduced an international style so that no matter where we are

from, or what land we come from, we have a common language to communicate with—the language of fashion.

One of my favorite quotes, which popped out of a fortune cookie at dinner one night, is by Oscar Wilde, who wrote,

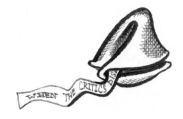

"When the critics disagree, the artist is in accord with himself." My parents and my upbringing taught me this same lesson: that authenticity is essential if you're going to live in harmony with yourself.

This philosophy is like the beauty of jazz. When jazz musicians are all jamming and playing from their inner emotions, you don't just hear the music. You feel it. In a similar way, your style flows naturally when who you are on the inside is in harmony with how you live your life on the outside. I give my inner voice expression through fashion. Weaving our personal stories together and expressing those stories helps define who we are as individuals.

UNDERSTANDING THE
BEAUTY OF QUALITY

In my father's store, my mother was
in charge of clerical duties and my
father was an ace salesman who earned
the complete trust of his clients. I believe that my
love of construction began in this store.

My favorite part of the store was the stockroom.
Whenever I visited the store, I spent hours there.
The stockroom was a smaller version of Home
Depot. For me, it was a magical place, like Willy
Wonka's Chocolate Factory. The shelves were stacked with
boxes of screws and rings in varied shapes for me to look at
and play with; I sometimes imagined that, if I could just figure
out how to put all of these intriguing bits of metal together, I
could build an entire house.

That stockroom was a treasure trove filled with amazing
objects that *did* things. The items each had a function and they
were all practical. My appreciation for all things practical,
logical, and well defined first took root at the hardware store.
It was there that I also first observed the geometric shapes that
would later become my pattern pieces: the circles, triangles,

spirals, and squares that could all fit together in different ways, like precise puzzles.

As a young girl, I loved to play with dolls, too, but I did so in a curious way: I would take them apart so that I could understand their inner workings, then put them together again. I remember when dolls went from having a rubber band construction where you could pull the arms and legs out from the torso without the limbs coming off, because the rubber bands acted like pulleys, to the moment when a socket-and-pressure system was introduced. Once this happened, if I pulled hard enough on the arms and legs of my dolls, the appendages came off completely. That change signaled to me—a girl of six—that the quality of my dolls was going downhill fast! Obviously, it was a move by manufacturers to produce cheaper dolls, but even as a child, I remember feeling that my dolls had lost an internal strength and mystery.

Today, my fascination with the insides of things, and with the ingenuity of how things are

constructed, remains at the core of my aesthetic. The beauty in the quality of an object surpasses the question of taste. Quality looks good even as it decays. This is why I say that, if you have the discipline, buy less, but buy better. If you can afford to buy the best, eventually pass it on, because it will most likely outlive you.

Understanding how something is built ensures that I can achieve my creative thought, thus reaching the highest quality in my designs.

THE VALUE OF CREATIVE CONTROL

Another important thing that I learned during my early childhood was the value of creative control and independence. The freedom to follow your instincts is a gift.

On rainy days as children in Camajuani, my sisters and I played with Mother Nature herself. We would try to outrun the sun showers that we could see approaching block by block. These warm showers fell hard and steadily from the sky, as if suddenly a faucet high above us had opened.

At home on those rainy days, my sisters and I also loved lying on the terrazzo floor of my grandmother's house facing the street and making paper boats. We would wait for just the right moment, when the rain suddenly stopped pouring down, and run outside. Then we would place our origami creations on the street curb so that we could watch them float down to the corner, carried on the small rivers of rainwater flooding the streets.

My lesson here was that bigger is not always better. Most of the time, the big boats collapsed under the raindrops while the little ones safely made it all the way to the end of the block. To this day, I have never forgotten the boat lesson. I try to keep my fashion business as hands-on as possible. A good business model means starting small, so that you can be prepared for

healthy growth. Each step in your growth should be small enough for you to manage it.

As a maker, how you shape something, even your business, can make or break your identity. It's not just the design that matters, but the manner in which you execute your design ideas. Understanding how things work ensures that I can achieve my creative vision with integrity.

DRESSING EMOTION

I have always thought of myself as a seamstress, as a maker of clothing, rather than a fashion person. I understand clothes from an abstract place that is not necessarily visual, but deep and emotional.

Sewing is where my innovations happen, and I love the techniques of sewing more than anything else. The seamstress knows fashion intuitively. This intimacy with the cloth and the act of making is evident in the garments themselves.

I don't start new things at the sketch pad or the drawing board. For me, fashion design begins at the sewing machine and the pattern-making table. I know that I am creating

a design when I make things with my
hands, giving them form and
shape, often inventing new
techniques to fold and
manipulate cloth as I
experiment with my designs
and perfect them over time.
This transformation cannot
happen with a sketch.

Understanding anatomy, body
language, and the space we inhabit
is crucial to my work. Before I can
envision how a dress will look or what
kind of fabric to use, I am compelled
to consider how the person who wears it
will feel when she puts on my garment. The
interaction between body and cloth creates an emotion, which
can affect the mood of the person wearing that garment.
Clothing can enhance our powers of communication, but only
if we feel comfortable within that second skin. In this sense,
fashion is a tool of self-expression that should set us free.

Dressing emotion goes both ways. Clothing can help the
wearer give voice to her emotions, whether she is feeling

vulnerable, sensual, confident, powerful, or playful. Certain garments can also look and feel so good on the body that they change how we feel when we wear them.

Growing up in a land very much in love with its endless curves made my frail-looking, pointy body incredibly evident. As a child, I was weightless and sharp like a needle, and the "shy" in me was born.

One day, I was intrigued by a conversation that my parents were having about a new vitamin injection that came from Russia and supposedly could make me grow stronger. The thought of a more rococo me was exhilarating. The idea that I might be able to shed my angular shape and grow curves made bearable my weekly visits to the kindly woman who would administer these shots.

I never gained those badly wanted pounds that the Russian shots promised to supply. Instead, I later came to rely on what I knew best, fashion, to camouflage my skinniness, as I observed my own body, tapped into my emotions, and experimented with my wardrobe. I would learn to make and layer my own clothes in ways that made me look and feel confident instead of appearing like a shy child.

WEAVING TOGETHER THE COLORS
AND TEXTURES OF MY CHILDHOOD

We are shaped and defined by our experiences. Our inner
landscapes are composed of the many sights, sounds, aromas,
and tactile sensations we absorb along the way. Cuba's diverse
environment prepared me to develop a global palette well
suited to creativity.

As a child, I listened to the soothing sounds of church bells
that were just as prominent as the chants of spiritual healers.
The variety of influences and personalities coexisted side by

side to make up a fascinating environment—all distinctly different, yet woven together with the fluid juxtaposition of an exotic braid. I did not have to go far to peek into other worlds.

One house over from ours, for instance, lived our neighbor Julia, who headed up the neighborhood watch group called Cuba's Committee for the Defense of the Revolution. Julia was the woman who had once saved my life by dunking me in ice cubes to bring my ultra-high fever down while my mother ran to get the doctor. She had ebony skin and wore immaculately pressed white cotton shirtdresses as strict and correct as the woman herself. She was tough, fair, and very aware.

To the left of our house lived Claudia, a lawyer, with her husband and son. What impressed me most about Claudia was the graphic and clear expression in her body language; her pale skin; and her perfectly groomed, pitch-black hair, which she kept brushed away from her face as she sat in her home office, surrounded by floor-to-ceiling shelves of leather-bound books.

Directly across the street lived germaphobic
Fronilde, her hands always placed high
near her chest, as though she might float
and protect herself from the growing
earth. Her skin was scaly and pearly white,
with matte red lipstick drawn in with
extra expressions. From her house always
escaped the most beautiful sounds of the
piano, which she played every afternoon.

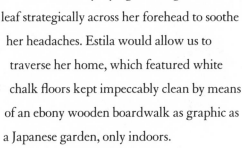

Right next door lived Estila. A tall and
regal mulatto woman, she wore her hair
stretched back in icy perfection and was cool
to look at even in the hot Caribbean sun. Gold
circles hung from her ears like quotation marks
and were especially well suited to her noble head, which she

further accessorized by laying a fresh green sabila
leaf strategically across her forehead to soothe
her headaches. Estila would allow us to
traverse her home, which featured white
chalk floors kept impeccably clean by means
of an ebony wooden boardwalk as graphic as
a Japanese garden, only indoors.

In my memory, Camajuani always
smelled of fruits, roses, and tobacco. We

used to happily follow Estila's boardwalk to her backyard, where we ate fruit from her mamonsillo tree. And around the corner from my grandmother's home lived two elderly Chinese brothers whose *traspatio* was linked to our backyard. Their magical garden gave fruit and vegetables in such abundance that during lean times we all ate from their vines.

Meanwhile, my aunt patiently tended and coaxed the roses in her garden to bloom again and again. The scent of her roses mingled with the tangy sent of lemons; she grew the lemon trees next to the roses to help ward off any insects that might invade her garden.

Even more pervasive than my aunt's roses and lemon tree was the aroma of tobacco leaves wafting from the town's *depsalillo*, a Colonial-era warehouse as big as an entire New York City block. This was one of my favorite places to walk past. All of its doors opened onto the street, and I could peer inside and see a vast, high ceiling that danced with the rhythmic movements of the spinning fans overhead.

Within this breezy space, women sat surrounded by mounds of beautifully dark tobacco leaves. The motions of the women separating and dissecting the leaves created a robotic, mesmerizing sound. The aroma of the wafting tobacco leaves was the perfume of the day. My favorite sight to witness was during the afternoon hour, when the work shift ended and a sea of women invaded the street, all with their own particular styles of tossing their sweaters around their shoulders, announcing the end of a hard day at work.

The women of Camajuani breathed style in a way that can't ever be taught. They exuded independence and control. These are the women whom I still remember today when I design and make clothes that fit well, and allow women to walk freely and purposefully down the street in full stride. Fueled with a strong sense of independence, the women of Camajuani exuded the power of women being in full command of themselves. Every time I watch a fashion show, I am consumed with the same powerful message.

Growing up and watching the women all around me express their emotions through clothing taught me that fashion can be an extension of your inner vision, reinforcing your individuality and style. This diversity, which I found all around me in Camajuani, is the wonderfully textured fabric of my childhood. Today, I use these memories and impressions, weaving my life experiences into my designs to make a strong foundation, just as many threads woven together make a strong cloth.

Camajuani was my town, and its people were my family. I
was nurtured by an entire city of women. Many years later, when
I started showing collections, *Paper* magazine's Kim Hastreiter
wrote in one of my earliest reviews that "these clothes are for
women who do not need men." When I read those lines, I knew
exactly what Kim meant. The cut of my early collections featured
fearless and imposing shapes, soft armor for strong women.

Independent women are definitely part of my DNA, despite
the fact that my natural beginnings were quite vulnerable: I
stayed in my mother's womb much too long, arriving at almost
the tenth month looking as long as a lizard and as wrinkled
as a prune. My grandmother used to say that I could only get
younger because I was born old.

In my work, Kim was able to extract an important essence
infused by my childhood. Since I was surrounded by my
mother's fifteen sisters all taking turns to help raise us, I had
a large pool of role models and a diversity of body types and
styles that exemplified the very idea of individuality.

The balance of threads woven together with different
tensions gives cloth its strength and integrity, just as my own
collections are woven from the threads of my own experiences.
Fashion is the weave of life itself, and can address and express
the fiber of the human soul.

Clothing can protect your vulnerabilities, enhance your
strengths, and highlight your potential. It can help you stand

out and be noticed. Or, if you choose, clothing can help you comfortably hide in plain sight, only you get to make the call. I love that fashion has the power to help us achieve mystery and create harmony with our inner and outer lives.

THE NATURE OF CREATIVITY: A LIFE OF RESOURCEFULNESS AND INVENTION

Through food, I learned about resourcefulness and inventiveness. I experienced taste or lack of taste from the exposure to a broad sensation to my palate, under the umbrella of nourishment. My taste buds were globalized in my early years, and it all started in my grandmother's kitchen. My grandmother Gregoria's cooking was famous in Camajuani even after the Revolution, when ingredients were scarce and a rich diet stood in defiance to the Revolution. "Make do" was always on the menu. I still enjoy stretching my creative juices with self-imposed limitations to kitchen ingredients.

I have always loved to cook, thanks to my grandmother, and I've also followed her example of making do. For my first collection in 1985, for instance, when money was so tight, I used mostly denim since it was the only fabric we could afford. I was already a fan of this durable cloth, first popularized in

America by gold miners in the mid nineteenth century, so I was thrilled to find unwanted yardage in brilliant colors due to its unfashionable status in high fashion at the time. It was the perfect textile to cut into the clean, sharp, structured shapes I was after. I essentially banished the casual hippie persona out of denim and kept all of its hardworking, double-stitched integrity.

In fact, Ruben and I have had some of our most creative moments during exactly those lean times when we needed to be the most resourceful. It isn't the abundance of choices and supplies that makes you creative, but the energy and originality you bring to the materials you have at hand.

When the Revolution began, the pigments of my landscape started to change. The tribe of girls who roamed my house and neighborhood were mostly made up of my own cousins and friends of my sisters. These girls were all tougher, bigger, and smarter than I was, and I recall feeling like I couldn't grow up fast enough. Little by little, all of my older cousins morphed, one by one, from flowers to fatigues. Their crispy cool summer dresses were replaced by olive green army uniforms.

This must have been a wake-up call for my parents, a very potent visual symbol that it was time to leave the country. The idea of militarized daughters in the future must have freaked them out. Even our house, formerly a bright white stucco, had to be painted olive green, I think because that was the only paint available.

By seventh grade, young girls and boys were being sent to mandatory farming camps in Cuba. My parents were understandably worried about the impact the Revolution would have on their three daughters. Like hundreds of thousands of other Cubans, they chose to leave their home and family and come to the United States to escape the effects of Castro's regime.

Although I left Cuba, I have always respected my roots. The authentic way that my parents lived their lives; my grandmother's resourcefulness and optimism; the diverse sights, sounds, and smells of a Colonial town; and the strong, fearless women of Camajuani all left powerful imprints on my soul that remind me of who I am and where I came from. My childhood experiences gave me the ability to be unflinching when it comes to discovering myself through art, taking creative risks, making tough business decisions that allow me to stay true to my vision, remaining independent, and mastering my own life.

2 Maintaining Roots and Origins in a New World

Everything I create is an extension of who I am and what I believe. This is why I rely on my intuition and feelings when I approach a design.

LANDING IN THE U.S. WAS VERY much like changing the television channel. One minute, you *comprende*, and the next moment, words take on abstract sounds. Upon our arrival at the airport, I was surrounded by incomprehensible sounds

and a bevy of new and exotic Americans. I
enthusiastically and instinctively absorbed
all of this new stimulation as I rapidly
mastered a new language, new customs, and
encountered new friends.

I plunged into the rush of these
experiences, exploring everything from rock
and roll to American slang, from unkempt
hair to embroidered blue jeans, as I embraced

my independence and freedom in a
new country. These quintessentially
American experiences became woven
into the complex, textured tapestry of
who I am as a designer today.

A WONDERLAND OF CARS, ESCALATORS, AND REVOLVING DOORS

The year of my arrival was 1968. Freedom, hippies, and automated doors were in the air, and to an eight-year-old, this air smelled like the future. I loved it. It was a year of transformations, antiwar demonstrations, political turmoil, and cultural upheaval all around the world.

In Cuba, the only things my sisters and I had learned about the U.S. came from the few images we had seen on the government-controlled television channels. These programs showed images of the race riots that were occurring in the U.S. at the time, and the frightening sights of the hoses and dogs being used to control crowds during protest marches as anti-American propaganda. For this reason, my grandmother preferred to listen to the radio instead, which informed the public hourly about which lottery numbers had been called for families eager to leave the country.

My sisters were older than I was, by two and three years, so they were old enough to comprehend and feel what changes life might hold for us in our new country. Being young, I mostly saw our departure for a new country as a great adventure waiting to happen. I was too young to understand that I would never see our town, our friends, or my beloved grandmother in our beautiful house again.

We were among the 450,000 Cubans who passed through Miami's Freedom Tower between 1962 and 1974. All Cuban refugees were met there by volunteers who provided translators, food, medical care, and financial support. We spent three days in this butter yellow building, modeled after Spain's Giralda Tower in Seville. Cubans everywhere referred to the Freedom Tower as "The Refuge," because it was here that most people from our country came first to sort out their new lives. It was our Ellis Island, and thinking of it still brings a flood of emotions and memories for most of us who immigrated at that time.

Our family was being sponsored by a cousin, a Vietnam vet in his twenties, who had escaped Cuba a few years before. He had already brought his mother and sister from the island to the U.S. We stayed in Miami, Florida, for only three days until we joined our cousin up north in New Jersey. He lived close to West New York, another haven for Cubans in the 1960s.

When we first arrived in Miami, I was struck most of all by the tall buildings and by how many cars there were, since most of the cars in our town had been confiscated during the Revolution, and people were once again relying on horses for transportation. I was also entranced by escalators and revolving doors.

Best of all, even as a child I was aware of a novel and exciting informality in the U.S. For instance, we never saw grown men and women wearing shorts as proper city wear in Cuba at that time, yet everyone in Miami seemed to wear them. In Cuba, too, there was no generation gap, in the sense that people of all ages did things together with their families. Teenagers enjoyed socializing with their families on weekends. In the U.S., I was amazed to see teenagers running around in tribes instead of hanging out with their parents. It was like suddenly being transported to some kind of wonderland, and that positive feeling I had when I first came to this country has stayed with me always.

. . .

MY FATHER SOON DECIDED TO move us to West New York, New Jersey. As we arrived in New Jersey and exited Newark Airport, heading east on the turnpike to our new home in West New York, I was struck by the welcoming sight of the Pulaski Skyway. This bridge, which opened in 1932 and was named after a Revolutionary War Polish general, connects two industrial towns, Newark and Jersey City. The steel and design of this cantilever bridge reminded me of my grandmother's sewing machine.

Because they were political refugees, my parents were allowed to work immediately. My father quickly found work in a mill that made knitted fabric, where I loved to visit and watch the machines all humming at once. My mother took a job in another factory that manufactured ignition parts for airplanes. She was soon very proud to announce that she was the fastest on the production line.

We moved into a fifth-floor walk-up apartment in West New York. Despite not having an elevator, I was thrilled to be living so high up in the sky, since in Camajuani there weren't any buildings taller than two stories. It was an old building with tall windows that let in great light. Our favorite game there was to lean out of the windows to catch balls that the neighborhood boys would throw up to us. My mother was terrified that we'd fall out of one of those windows, compelling her to rapidly learn her first words in English: "That's all finish, Boy!"

I loved my new life because I felt such a sense of freedom. As a young girl, I was always so energetic—always riding my bike or playing ball, and scarcely ever sitting still even in the house—that my mother called me her "little grasshopper." The only school award I ever won, in fact, was for "class athlete" because the sensation of movement was so stimulating to me.

I loved running, jumping, dancing, or anything else that gave me a sense of freedom, power, and independence. Later, I would incorporate that feeling of joy in movement into clothes I made for women. I want every woman to be able to walk confidently, with her true powerful stride, when she wears my designs.

NEW LOOKS FOR THE U.S.

Although we arrived in the U.S. in the summer and the
weather wasn't so different from Cuba, the feeling of my new
home was completely distinct. I had never been surrounded
by so many tall buildings, not to mention the spectacular and
overwhelming view of Manhattan, which was presented to us
daily on the silver platter known as the Hudson River.

At night, the city took on the added glamour of a million
lights, transforming it into something as magical as the
Emerald City in *The Wizard of Oz*, or some metropolis in a
futuristic movie. The sunlight reflected differently in West
New York as a result of the majestic Hudson, and I became
aware of new shadows and architectural shapes.

In the 1970s and 1980s, West New York became a little
Havana on the Hudson, as more and more Cuban refugees
migrated north from Miami. The town was revitalized by this
influx of people, who gave new life to commerce. A bustling
new scene sprang up to accommodate the social customs that
had always been part of our daily lives in Cuba, only with a
much larger population. Instead of living in a small, sleepy
town, where time seemed to stretch out forever, America was
a roller-coaster ride. I felt a fast urban beat—so many cars and

people!—and I was excited to be in such a busy and gritty place and surrounded by so many unfamiliar faces on the streets.

My father, however, wanted his three daughters growing up in a quieter neighborhood. He soon moved us out of that apartment and into a rental house on a tree-lined street just a few blocks away. This house had a yard and terraces overlooking the town stadium, a perfect place for us to absorb the fascinating American cultural rituals of football, marching bands, cheerleaders, and parades through our backyard fence.

Much of my cultural education in the U.S. came courtesy of television and the *TV Guide*. We watched anything and everything on TV, thrilled by the novelty of so many different programs after the tired political propaganda on Cuban television. From Bugs Bunny to *Soul Train*, from *American Bandstand* to Fellini films on Channel 13, it was a rich diet of entertainment and information.

We had years of pop culture catching up to do, not only because we were new to the country, but because in Cuba we had been so isolated during the Revolution. My mom, a great fan of the movies and of all things entertaining, became an early subscriber to the television bible of the day: *TV Guide*. Through television programs and movies, we learned about the wide scope of American womanhood, from Barbara Stanwyck's frontier woman's gutsy bravado to Bette Davis's sharp, attenuated movements, and from Lauren Bacall's tough-dame gestures to Katharine Hepburn's relaxed, sophisticated body language.

The American woman, I learned, could be funny, tough, intelligent, sophisticated, flirty, hilarious, practical, athletic, and downright dangerous. The scope of moods and lifestyle in our new homeland, at least as portrayed in the movies, offered me a rich, liberating variety of role models to choose from. Musicals, Westerns, film noir, and romantic comedies all informed my blossoming sense of style.

Our first Christmas in the States, I was thrilled to get a spinning ballerina doll. My oldest sister got a radio, and my other sister received a portable record player. At about the same time, our beloved *TV Guide* offered a subscription service where you could order the latest hit record albums for a mere ninety-nine cents each! We excitedly signed up for this service, but since we could barely read English, we missed the fine print that explained how you had to cancel the subscription to this cavalcade of albums, or else they would automatically be delivered to your house.

Innocence is bliss. We were overjoyed, if a little bewildered, by this sudden bounty, as a mother lode of new record albums promptly appeared at our doorstep every week. Into my life stepped Janis Joplin, Jimi Hendrix, Herman's Hermits, the

Beatles, Joan Baez, Bob Dylan, the Woodstock Trilogy Album, and the Who—everything that a young girl needed to learn how to become an American teenager!

The sudden influx of so many U.S. influences from television and music caused a nearly instant transformation in my sisters and me as we layered on our new American selves. For my oldest sister, Any, that meant wearing her hair in long, Native American–like braids on either side of her head and draping ponchos over her clothes. My middle sister, Mary, was more of a hot pants, James Brown kind of girl with a little bit of a Tina Turner and Stevie Nicks attitude.

For me, it was long, dreary plaid coats and turtlenecks for a *Shaft* meets *Superfly* effect. This was just great for riding my sled in the snow! My mom could deal with my fashion transformation because it at least kept me warm, but my new long, stringy, face-hiding hair was just too much of an unkempt mess, in her opinion. Luckily, the movie *Love Story* saved the day, because my mom could relate to Ali MacGraw's knitted cap pulled neatly over her ears—and over her long straight hair.

I LEARNED TO SPEAK ENGLISH rather quickly, in part due to the easy way kids have of mimicking and picking up mannerisms and languages. The new albums really came in handy in that

department. They allowed me to pick up a whole lot of pop wisdom from those poetic lyrics. My friend Pearl, who was also a new arrival from my hometown in Cuba, and I would lip-synch to Michael Jackson's "ABC" in our matching zip-front jumpsuits. I adored the look and freedom of jumpsuits, because they conceal your body while revealing your body language at the same time. For me, a jumpsuit is the perfect work wear, utility at its best. To this day, I make sure that there are always a few such garments in each of my collections.

In a way, my sisters and I were living a double life, like so many children of immigrants, and I enjoyed the variety of it. Our parents tried their best to keep our home life orderly and as close as possible to what we had known in Cuba, to provide us with some sense of normalcy and continuity. We still spoke Spanish at home and ate many of the same Cuban foods, sitting down every night to share a meal. This meant eating at seven or even eight p.m., after our parents were home from work, as we had always done in Cuba, instead of at six p.m. like so many of our native-born American classmates.

At home, too, a certain formality was the norm and elegance was defined by good behavior. We had rules that many American teenagers didn't have to follow then, and certainly don't today, like no hanging out in the bedrooms. Beds were for sleeping, not for sitting and chatting with friends. Your bedroom was not an office, clubhouse, or studio. "It's not sanitary," my mother explained. "You should leave the street grime outside."

As the children of two hardworking immigrant parents, we were also expected to do chores that went beyond just making our beds: It was our responsibility to help run the household. As the youngest, I got off easy, but I saw my older sisters pick up the basic essentials of life, like starting dinner and doing laundry, without ever being taught to do so.

There were still the same important cultural rituals, too, like the baptisms and *quinceañeras*, a custom my parents were happy to see me avoid like the plague. Once in a while there were weddings, too. Old habits die hard, and on weekends we went to these celebrations in rented halls, or we socialized and went to dances in the many Cuban social clubs and other venues that had started springing up all over New Jersey to accommodate Cuban immigrants. These events always sold out to capacity. The enthusiasm and love for dancing and socializing was so strong that this scene attracted the likes of such musical legends as Celia Cruz, Tito Puente, The Fania All Stars, Tipica 73 and many other legendary musical groups.

In Latin cultures, there is no generation gap when it comes to dancing and socializing. The entire family tree participates in these traditions and rituals—from the grandmothers all the way down to the youngest kids. In fact, it is often the elders in the clan who really have the best moves, the most clever twists and turns. The couples who have danced together the longest can outshine the brightest on the dance floor. These gatherings were something you look forward to as a kid—the idea that one day, you and your partner can create the most beautiful dance. I attended these weekly excursions with my sisters and parents from a very young age, which was a good way to try to outgrow my shyness.

In the summer, caravans of newly arrived Cuban families, including my own, took excursions to the beach, the lakes, or the big state parks. People you may not have known back home now became your new family in the States. America's outdoor life felt grand and exotically free, because of the enormity and variety of the landscape, not to mention the magic and novelty of witnessing the four seasons.

Away from home, in the part of our life not necessarily shared with our parents, my sisters and I raced to catch up with our American peers as quickly as possible. We spoke English at school and absorbed American teen mannerisms, street slang, and foods. Since I was such an active child, I used sports and street games as a great excuse to stay outdoors until my mother or sisters came looking for me. The entire street was my playground.

In a way, the American experience for me had a great deal to do with a new sense of independence, simply because every day, we came home from school and had to fend for ourselves until our parents came home from work. We were no longer in a small town where everyone knew me and my family. There were no more aunts or grandmothers to look after us. We were on our own. This was a very liberating feeling, and a catalyst for anticipating and accepting responsibility for yourself.

I discovered the Hula-hoop around then, which is still one of my favorite activities today. I can still swing the Hula for hours, getting lost in this perfect circular motion. This feeling of freedom and movement are strong design directives for me. Even when I'm making an evening dress, the playfulness and freedom of circular shapes is often a key element in my designs.

A SEAMSTRESS IS BORN

For the first year we were in the States, my oldest sister was in charge of us after school. When I was about to enter fourth grade, though, my mother decided that we needed someone else to keep an eye on us until she got home from work in the evening. Instead of informing us that we would have a babysitter—an announcement that surely would have caused us to rebel—my clever mother told us that we were going to take sewing lessons from a seamstress after school.

I looked forward to these sessions. At first, this kindly neighbor taught me to make stuffed animals. I sat at her dining room table with fabric that she had already cut into shapes, and she taught me how to hand-stitch the seams and stuff the animals. It wasn't long before I was asking to use her sewing machine. I still remembered the magic of that mysterious sewing machine at my grandmother's house in Cuba, and I was determined to master it even at age nine.

Looking back on things now, I imagine that the babysitter, who was probably desperately trying to fix dinner for her own family at the same time that she was taking care of us, was probably annoyed when I kept wanting to learn more. But, either out of the goodness of her heart or because I showed so much interest and asked her so many times, she eventually gave in and taught me how to use her machine.

My father had bought a Singer sewing machine for our household soon after moving to New Jersey. This was odd, in a way, because I never saw my sisters or my mother use it. My father was always fond of tools—he always had a fully equipped toolbox, and I'm sure that I must have inherited my love of tools from him—so maybe he bought it thinking that every house should have one, just like every house should have a hammer and a set of screwdrivers.

In any case, I, too, have come to believe that a sewing machine is a household fixture that nobody should ever have to live without. If you make room for it, it will get used. A sewing machine contains curiosity, mystery, and, in my case, a certain respect, especially if you can get it to run. In our house, I was the one who dared to venture over to sit at the sewing machine, and so it became mine.

I suppose one reason that I wanted to learn how to use that machine so badly is because I couldn't find any ready-made clothes that fit me or made me feel the way I wanted to feel. I was awkwardly long and thin. It didn't help that I had two older sisters whose bodies were already developing curves, while at age ten, I couldn't even wear the same clothes that other girls my age wore, much less clothes as grown-up as theirs.

To find clothing that fit me, so far I'd had the best luck shopping in the young children's sections of the department stores. For example, one of my favorite outfits at that time consisted of a smock dress made for a very young child, with matching bloomers that I rolled up like shorts. I had also tried to camouflage my way-too-skinny frame by layering shorts over shorts, and by wearing skirts over pants, among many other experiments with ready-to-wear clothing.

I desperately wanted to make clothing that looked like it actually fit me. I was tired of wearing clothes that were too big, and I felt silly shopping for children's clothes. I also wanted to wear clothing that didn't look "Mama-made," but manufactured and store-bought. By age eleven, I realized that I would get clothing that fit me only if I made it myself.

The first pattern I ever bought was a Simplicity pattern for a tent dress. I made the dress out of a taupe linen-rayon blend because the fabric seemed very grown-up to me, and topstitched it in brown thread because I wanted to see every line of that dress outlined, like a drawing. Of course, the dress had pockets, too. Even from an early age, I always wanted to wear clothes that were intelligently practical as well as beautiful.

I felt wonderful when I put on that tent dress. It fit me, it wasn't a little girl's dress, and it was exactly the right style for my state of mind. The new me was starting to hatch. This was the beginning of my true understanding of how clothing can transform your image—and serve your emotions. All you need to have on hand to create a fresh vision for yourself are the most basic tools: a sewing machine, a needle and thread, scissors, a ruler, pins, and of course the willing model.

LEARNING TO SEW BECAME MY obsessive hobby and transformed my life. I immediately grasped the power that sewing had to enable me to communicate who I was. Before learning to complete truly worthy garments, I sharpened my sewing skills and stretched my creativity in simpler ways. I would create elaborate embroideries on my jeans, for instance, using pop culture images like an upside-down 7UP bottle with butterfly wings, or a peace sign with extra veins at its iconic roots.

This was also the first time that I thought to embroider the words on my back jeans pocket that I still believe in today: "The World Has No Seams." To me, this meant that we were all connected—all nationalities, all cultures. As a new immigrant, that was a powerful message. I was, in my young mind, owning and living the times, and using my jeans as a canvas to artfully convey my thoughts and ideas.

Now, as I began to master the sewing machine, it was as if I were suddenly in the driver's seat of my own life. I could go anywhere from now on!

Probably nothing is more symbolic of that period of my life than the dress I made in seventh grade home economics class. This was a shirtwaist dress in a great, slinky rayon fabric in a bright Hawaiian print of terra-cotta, blue, and green. The fabric was so soft that it felt like skin.

The dress had puffy sleeves and a belt; I wore it with impossibly high platform shoes and felt fabulously grown-up. At last, I thought I looked like a teenager, and I loved it. I was still skinny and awkward looking, but I was dressing the changes happening in my mind even before my physical transformation had really begun.

From that point on, I focused on buying dress patterns of my own. I reused them over and over again, putting them together in different ways, forming my own combinations and altering them ever so slightly as I began to understand the fundamentals of pattern making. I was enthralled by these giant paper patterns that were folded into envelopes like origami and printed with geometric shapes that I could cut along the dotted lines to make three-dimensional objects. Even the patterns were sensitive works of art to me.

I spent hours picking out the smartest patterns from those grand, weighty books of Vogue, McCall's, and Simplicity patterns. I loved space, and the feeling of space. The curve of a wall might make me think about the curve in a garment. To me, clothing patterns were like blueprints that architects use. I could easily imagine how those flat patterns would fall onto my body, and think, "Wow. This transforms into a dress!" Much later, when one of my patterns was featured on the cover of a Vogue pattern book in July/August 1995, I experienced a thrill as I realized that I had fulfilled an ambition that I didn't even know I had as a little girl.

At this point in my life, I was still constantly searching for new ways to make myself look older and more developed, like my sisters and even like other girls my age. Adolescence was happening to the girls all around me, but had bypassed me so far. I tried to accelerate, or at least jump-start, the process by continuing to cut my hair shorter and shorter. I started to wear platform sandals, which only exaggerated my long, disproportionate assemblage of limbs. Not only were my legs too long, but my hands practically hung next to my knees. I continued to tweeze my eyebrows until they looked as thin as pencil lines. I was determined to become a lady.

Every day after school, I would sit down at that machine and sew something. My newly acquired skills gave me confidence and freedom. My oldest sister's classic clothing provided me with the perfect fabrics and styles for experimenting and expanding my sewing skills, as I cut the clothing apart and remade it to suit my awkward frame.

She had expensive taste even at a young age and a well-trained eye for quality and for picking out the best of the classics. Her collection of cotton shirts were dreamy enough to inspire me to design shirts I would call "Brooke Sisters." I took to cruising her potential hand-me-downs, patiently plotting their redesign in my mind.

My sister's plaid blazer would become my double-breasted jumper dress, and I turned her gray flannel trousers into a drawstring skirt. I'd cut the bottoms off shirts, and wrap the severed hems as cords around my body, so that the shirts would taper in to fit me with the sleeves remaining big and flowing. Cutting apart and reappropriating talents were perfected with the help of my big sister's castaways.

Whenever I was running out of hand-me-downs to remake, I would start hunting down great finds in the army and navy stores and in the now-defunct Woolworth's, places where you could find good quality work clothes, which are the foundation of great American sportswear. I learned to apply my eye for glamour to practicality as I searched for the rare find in a forest of the mass produced.

In a sea of blue jeans, I would fish out the one pair of chambray denim jeans from the 1950s with a side zipper. Or I would find the red wide wale corduroy tube leg jeans, the super-high-waisted dark indigo sailor pants, or the oversized and perfectly tailored peacoat in a warm felted wool. In this way, I developed my antennae for newness and my appreciation for difference. In fact, it was more like irregulars crying out to be found. I had a gift for finding in a sea of sameness the odd man out.

My parents didn't quite know what to make of this. I remember my father sitting in what Ruben would later call "the inquisition La-Z-Boy chair" and waiting for me to exit my bedroom, dressed in whatever latest outfit I'd crafted. He always wore an approving, amused look, no matter how experimental my outfits.

My mother, on the other hand, just shook her head in confusion, resigned to having such a rebellious daughter. Nonetheless, she would feel compelled to ask, "Why can't you just make a pretty little dress?"

This was my earliest experience of engaging others in my craft as I began to discover, build, and sharpen my design vision, and I loved it. I also made dresses for my sisters: gauzy smock and wrapped jersey dresses, or topstitched, slinky dresses that were far too adult and sexy for me to carry off. I would have to wait to grow into that part of me, but I loved making dresses for my sisters, because it allowed me to test out my ideas and see how they worked on others.

MAKING CLOTHES WITHOUT RULES

Because I knew nothing about sewing, I made my first clothes with no rules at all, except that the clothing had to be both comfortable and well anchored to my body. I had none of the basic dressmaker's tools yet—no dressmaker's form, carbon paper, tracing wheel, fabric weights, or pattern hooks—so I would simply drape fabric over my own body. I essentially used myself as a mannequin to see how certain lines and shapes would look and feel.

Since I had no rules, I was free to experiment. I would relocate traditional seams on a jacket, for instance, so that I would have more freedom of movement in my arms. As an experiment, I removed the seams from the crotch of my jeans and replaced them with jersey inserts. I was as interested in how the clothes felt on my body as I was in how they looked.

This is still true today. I like to make clothes that capture movement. That's why I never make a straight cut for a dress, for instance. I prefer a continuous, aerodynamic sort of line. If a line looks too meandering or not precise in a pattern, I instantly notice it and ask my pattern makers to "take the belly out" of the shape to give the pattern a smoother, cleaner line.

Finally, after several months of deconstructing my sister's garments and transforming them, I felt confident enough to cut my first original pattern and design something from scratch: a pair of pants. The most important aspect of my first design was what I managed to do without! I made a design with no industrial closures—no zipper, no buttons, or button fly. The sophistication of those finishes was way beyond my years. It was a pair of pants with extensions that wrapped around my body to hold them closed. I was very proud of my achievement, and of the ingenuity that had gone into thinking my way through the idea while sewing. It is still this way with me: Sewing is where my innovations happen, not at the drawing board or sketch pad.

By high school, except for my dependable Levi's and classic white shirts, I was creating almost every article of clothing I wore. I had become so enthralled with my personal design voice that I had my own little sweatshop going on all by myself. My Singer home sewing machine never took a break. I worked nonstop, sewing seven days a week to craft outfits for myself and work out new design ideas. I did this almost by instinct. I was like an athlete in training, preparing myself for the grueling schedule of Fashion Week to come later on in my life.

Through maintaining my roots and origins in a new world while I learned to navigate the freer, more independent lifestyle of an American child and young teenager, I added key lessons about mobility, flexibility, and risk-taking to what I had already absorbed during my Cuban childhood. When I speak with young designers today, I encourage them to rely on their intuition and feelings when approaching a new design, because everything you create is an extension of who you are and what you believe.

Everything I learned as a child helped me become a more creative, professional maker, from Hula-Hooping to dancing with my family at Cuban parties on weekends, from reveling in American pop culture to learning how to sew for my own pleasure alone at home. You never know which experiences will be the most creatively useful as you solve new design problems. That's why it's so essential to be able to tap into the deepest parts of yourself and use them all.

3 Fashioning a Young Life

Fashion is communication. Whether it's a look or a lifestyle you're discovering, your creativity is your song. It's a gift to yourself, first, and then to the world.

FASHION IS ABOUT MUCH MORE than just clothes. It's about finding and defining yourself, and communicating your personality and individuality to other people through your outward appearance. In making my own clothes as a young teenager, I was essentially fashioning my life. Discovering for myself that clothing is communication, and combining this realization with the body language of dance, really allowed me to find my own center.

In my case, fashion helped me announce my new, more mature emotional identity even before my body began to transform into the grown-up version of me. Through experimentation, I discovered a love of art, music, and dance that would influence me for the rest of my life. By exploring and sharing my interests, I slowly began merging art into my everyday existence, as I started to fully embrace my creative talents and share them with the world.

HAIR REVOLUTION-EVOLUTION

Hair is our natural-born fashion accessory. A glorious, organic hat, our hair is usually our earliest encounter with fashion, and one which we all share. We learn to shape it, form it, and yank it into our ideal as soon as we can use a comb and discover the mirror. We take responsibility for our appearance through our hair message.

Whether our hair is kept or unkept, long or short, it tells our story. For most of us, women and men, too, having a truly satisfying haircut is important to how we look and feel. A woman's hair is often the first thing she notices about herself when she looks in the mirror, even when she's trying on new clothes.

Naturally, with a houseful of four women—my mother, myself, and my two sisters—hair was an omnipresent topic of interest and debate. My long, stringy hair continued to meet with resistance from my mother, who did not approve of such a subversive adolescent fashion statement.

She finally won that battle, but it is to my oldest sister that I owe my first real salon cut. Somehow, in that amazing way in which kids learn to sniff out a hip scene, my sister, Any, heard of a groovy hair salon in Greenwich Village. The building had painted white bricks and so many green fern plants hanging in the bay windows that one barely had a way to peek inside, and there was great music oozing out of the walls. Into that salon we all went with our willing mother, who was only too happy to see us being pruned and groomed to look like civilized young ladies.

Like my sisters, I got a haircut that day, but not just any haircut. This haircut had been years in the making, because in Cuba as children, our hair was kept short, neat, and well groomed. Since my arrival in the U.S., I had managed to keep it long. Now, at age eleven, I was ready for the change that I was trying to conjure up.

In Greenwich Village that day, I had my hair cut to look like the healthy, sultry tresses of Veronica Lake, or like the hair of some fearless dame from a film noir movie, but with a bit of Mary Hartman humor. I was amazed by how different I felt. Almost instantly, I became OK with grooming. It was an early lesson in how hair is a catalyst for change.

Even longer lasting than that hairstyle was the impression that Greenwich Village hair salon left on me, with its multicolored posters and people, the sounds of the exotic music blaring from the loudspeakers, the flow of the space, and the overall hip atmosphere. I was too young to be part of this moment, but the moment never left me. All of this adds up to what makes fashion so contagious: Fashion needs a life, and life creates fashion.

In that hair salon, I experienced fashion as culture for the first time. I saw how music and the flow of space, how the very atmosphere of a place can all be ingredients that make fashion so tangible and pertinent. I began to understand on a deeper level that fashion is a way to express yourself when you're leading a busy, multidimensional life. It allows you to say more with less. Mastering a fluency in fashion can help you broaden your horizons.

THROUGHOUT HIGH SCHOOL, I CONTINUED to cut my hair shorter and shorter, because it seemed more mature and sophisticated to me. Along with the new and improved grown-up version of me came more new hair adventures. My middle sister, Mary, introduced me to a new hair stylist in town, an Italian kid called Frankie G. who was very talented and enthusiastic about cutting hair. Although I wasn't looking for a new do, whenever I accompanied my sister to get her hair cut, Frankie G. roped me into getting mine cut, too. This was the start of a haircut-athon, as influential and as full of expression as the experience I'd had with the cavalcade of record albums years before. Frankie had a Vidal Sassoon–like talent for cutting hair with great precision and letting it do its thing, which was my type of cut. I didn't like to spend a lot of time on my hair. I didn't want to use a hair dryer every day to get my hair to cooperate. I have always been fearless with my hair, and with Frankie's help, I went from a Mary Hartman–meets–Veronica Lake do look to a Keith Richards look, an off-kilter Che Guevara beret haircut, a supersonic wedge, and an Iggy Pop electric lightbulb look. It got to be that I developed a fear of Frankie.

Whenever I was trying to let my hair
grow out, Frankie couldn't resist trying
out a new cut. I trusted his artistic
scissors and was open to the creative
collaboration. I contributed my hair,
and Frankie perfected his craft. By
allowing Frankie to experiment on
my hair, I was helping someone else find
his way toward realizing his artistic potential.
From this fertile ground in West New
York/New Jersey also comes one of my
favorite hair artists of all time, Orlando Pita,
another Cuban refugee. To this day, I am a
big believer in artistic collaborations, and in
contributing somehow to helping others
find their directions in life. It is fulfilling
and inspiring for me to watch others bloom.

THE TRIBAL ART DANCE

From the neighborhood house parties and Spanish social club
dances I had attended with my parents, I eventually graduated

to discos. I was recruited by my sisters; better yet, I was enlisted
by my parents to serve as an unofficial chaperone when my
sisters when out on dates. Since my parents had introduced
me to socializing at parties and halls, they encouraged me to
develop this side of me.

Going to discos with my sisters allowed me a new and
amazing freedom. I also became an excellent disco dancer,
winning many a hustle contest. Because I was light on my
feet and loved to dance, I became a much sought-after dance
partner. Really good disco dancing and the Latin hustle are
very demanding workouts. I loved physical movement and
was a natural-born athlete, so all-night dance marathons were
a natural extension of the former me, only in the skimpiest
high heels and looking just a bit more polished and slick.

I was once again thrilled to be living a double life. On
weekend nights, I was an aspiring adolescent disco dancing diva,
participating in dancing competitions and winning cash prizes.
By Monday morning, I returned to being a typical eighth grader,
one who loved the outdoors and playing ball in the street with
the neighborhood kids.

After dancing my way through most of New Jersey, the
next stop was Manhattan. These were the early days of disco,
when dance culture was still experimental and disco music was
reaching its height. The DJ was king, one-part artist, one-part

musician, and one-part poet, creating the mood for an entire
night. Music was mixed and blended to create sounds that
were as novel and stimulating to the ear as art was to the eyes.
I was only fourteen, and if not for my handiwork with
the sewing machine, I might not have experienced the
transformation that was taking place culturally in our society.
Because I had an original look, experimenting with fashion
and design from my hair to my clothes, I was able to gain
entry into discos, past the velvet ropes guarded by the keepers
of the doors.

This was a great achievement for an eighth grader from
New Jersey. I became the ticket for older boys from my
neighborhood to get into these clubs; without me, these
wonderfully sweet Jersey boys might never have been allowed
entry into clubs like Infinity, Xenon, or Studio 54. In return,
they provided me with transportation.

The New York dance club scene was like art gallery
openings, galas, vaudeville, and concerts all rolled into
one. It was where all of the major and minor arts met and
collaborated, including fashion, all generating ideas and
sparking off new impulses, as if we were in a giant laboratory
for experimenting and creating culture.

Besides great music and inspired dancers of all sizes,
stripes, and ages, the clubs provided the most wonderful

people watching on the planet. The magic of this time, which was long before VIP rooms, was that the clubs were truly democratic places that attracted everyone from the most famous stars to a bridge and tunnel teenager like me. You didn't even need to have a conversation. Everyone was there on the same wavelength and on the same thrilling amusement ride. There was an unscripted accessibility, with everyone sharing in the dance experience just by being there.

In these places, I first encountered some of the most legendary personalities in fashion, like the prolific Karl Lagerfeld. Little did I know then that Karl would one day photograph Ruben and me for one of our first museum exhibition catalogs. He was also the first to call me a couturier, a compliment that I don't take lightly, especially coming from someone of his knowledge and experienced eye. Among Karl's many talents is his never-failing ability to pick up on the new and the next.

I first saw fashion designer Thierry Mugler looking like a mythic Vulcan king in his long, menacing, Darth Vader–like cape. Thierry's otherwise ominous appearance was betrayed by the good nature evident in the sparkle of mischief in his eyes. His fashion notes were so operatic and futuristic that it's no wonder he has captivated the design world since the late 1970s with his structured, hyper-feminine clothing.

Thierry's costumes and the many collaborations with our
friend Joey Arias have been creative as well as technical
breakthroughs.

This was also the first time we encountered Bill Cunningham,
who later became a trusted and valued friend. Ruben calls him
the "Weegee of Fashion," always the first on the scene, capturing
the aura and halo of fashion movements. Bill's third eye points
him toward fashion and society's unknown energy as it suddenly
takes form. I didn't know then that Bill's talent for capturing the
Zeitgeist of fashion was so keen and pure that, for him, even some
teenagers from New Jersey could be interesting specimens for his
anthropological studies and ongoing documentation of Fashion
Life on Planet Earth.

It was Bill Cunningham who would later give us our very
first valuable advice when Ruben and I started presenting our
collections: "Keep your enthusiasm, kids," he said to us both one
day, as he spotted us walking down 57th Street, and that is one of
life's truest lessons. If you can stay in love and keep your enthusiasm
for what you choose to do with your life, you are living well indeed.
Always keep in mind that patterns in life repeat themselves, so
make a decision to own the patterns you want to keep.

Through the freedom and trust I had earned at home, I was
lucky to be able to spread my wings and fly into such enriching
territories at such a young and impressionable age.

For people who didn't grow up in such a social and tightly knit community as I did, it may seem odd that I was given this much freedom at a young age. However, in many ways, this was a natural transition for my sisters and me. It was part of the complete education that you can get only at home from your parents. You learn valuable lessons little by little as you observe your parents, extended family, and friends interacting in a relaxed and genuine manner, and you become prepared to deal with many personality types, and to be accepting and curious about differences.

Taking responsibility for yourself as you come of age happens step-by-step. My parents always taught my sisters and me to be self-reliant; to treat ourselves and everyone we encountered with respect; and to navigate the world with instinct, confidence, and a solid trust in humanity. My immigrant Cuban community provided me with an invisible safety net as I was growing up, even without me knowing it, until I felt ready to explore further. My parents were totally cool about letting us expand our social horizons, just as long as we got home around midnight. Since both Mom and Dad knew just about everyone in town, and their children, our home had a very open-door policy.

In hindsight, this was a smart tactic on my father's side. As the father of three girls, this was a wise way to be. He didn't build a moat and isolate his three daughters inside a castle to protect us from the world. Instead, he opened the gates so that all of the kids in the neighborhood, including the boys, could come into our home. My father commanded respect and gained the trust of all of the young, would-be suitors in town. By the time they came calling for permission to take my sisters out on a date, these young men knew that they had to gain my father's trust and live up to his standard of being responsible young men for him to grant that permission. The boys respected him; therefore, my father knew that they would respect his daughters.

GOING OUT ON WEEKENDS BECAME my passion and the reason that I became so prolific at cutting and sewing my own clothes on a regular basis. I stopped acquiring my sisters' useful hand-me-downs and began making fashion for my own consumption full-time. I took to tailoring fleece and hand-embroidering an entire spider's web with thread. I made bubble dresses out of light-as-air tulle held up with invisible fishing wire, and I sewed together and patch-worked all sorts of crocheted doilies and small lace handkerchiefs bought in thrift shops to make romantic circle skirts that were like delicate collages of antique textiles, pairing them with irregular white Hanes T-shirts.

At this time, I also developed a taste for vinyl. I made white vinyl jodhpurs skirts and futuristic funnel dresses worn with prim and proper nurse's shoes from the 1940s. Soon enough, I was mixing vinyl with lace.

Then came the challenge of sewing real leather. This was when my father bought me my first industrial sewing machine. It had been previously used in a coat factory, and now I had a tool of the trade! This would be the same sewing machine that I would use to start my career a few years later, and it is always in use at my studio today.

Everything I made, I would drape and experiment with on my own body, since I didn't have a dress form. This was to

be my biggest resource for inspiration. The
dialogue that my body experienced
with the cloth created visual
emotions that I attempted
to dress by wrapping,
tying, folding, and
crisscrossing
fabric. I
discovered new
silhouettes and
proportions
along the
way, and new
pattern shapes
particular to this
intimate way of
draping. I could never

have dreamed up these designs unless I was sewing them and making my own patterns.

Our bodies are much more than a front and a back; we are three-dimensional. We are formed in the round, made up of many angles and surfaces. By working in the round on my own body, I learned to do away with the basic side seams found in most of the store-bought patterns I had used while learning to sew.

When I displaced seams from the traditional sides, it was not so much a style choice as a logical solution that would allow me to more closely mimic my movements. I had taught myself to drape in motion. I recall the freeing feeling, like removing the training wheels of a bike, as I worked out shapes that resembled three-dimensional versions of the flat paper patterns I had first loved when I started sewing. All of this playing around would one day become my language and my complete body of work. I was learning how to communicate emotions visually, because I was always trying to design clothes that captured a feeling. As I touched on before, dressing emotion is one of the key motivations for my work to this day.

I really enjoyed making things with my hands and thinking my way through a design problem, like having too little fabric, not enough time, or no access to an industrial closure like a zipper. All innovations happen through problem solving. When you start to build your vision, to sew your first designs, the unexpected problem appears. How you navigate around this roadblock is where innovation is born and where you discover your identity as a designer.

AS A YOUNG SEAMSTRESS, FINDING fabrics that moved well and flowed with my body language became my ideal. Dancing inspired me to create a freedom of movement in clothing and the ability to read an attitude. This is still true when I look at women on the street: I notice the intelligence of a woman's body language first, not her clothes.

When you are a creator, copying other people's designs is never an option. I continued to create new forms in fabric. My work at the sewing machine grew increasingly more complex, in keeping with the broadening of my experiences and the artistic stimulation of the dance scene. I was beginning to find my way as a designer, though I didn't know it.

Key to my development was a deep respect for fabric. When I see a fabric, I connect with it because I feel what it can do. Fabric speaks to me. I have an emotional connection to fabric, as most women do, though too few of us are open to that soulful connection. If you allow it, fabric, like a song, can touch you deeply.

I began my dialogue with cloth using the most basic, easy-

to-handle weaves, primarily well-behaved cottons and linens.
I experimented with these fabrics by removing threads or
embroidering them with patchwork pieces of the same fabric.
Gradually, I ventured into crepes, crepe de chine, and charmeuse
fabrics. Each type of cloth represented a different me. Years
later, as I started using jersey, I was a pro at dedicating myself to
a fabric until I understood its true character.

Whenever I created a garment, I discovered that often I
had to look at the cloth, touch it, and listen to it. I still do this.
I watch the way gravity tugs at it or plays with it. And, in my
mind, I begin moving the fabric in different ways to see what
it can do. Ruben says that I have a mind like a computer, and
that I think like an architect in this way, or the way a sculptor
does, in three dimensions.

Watching fabric fall, or holding it against my body and
letting it drape, tells me a lot about the cloth and what can be
done with it. In a sense, what I do is try to grasp the deepest
essence of each fabric, allowing it to do what it is woven to do,
rather than trying to impose my will on it and torture it into
doing something alien to the fabric's true nature.

Even now, as then, I don't design on a notepad because I
need to think with my hands. The cloth directs me, not the
other way around. I am at the mercy of the weave. I learned
at an early age to surrender to the nature of the cloth, and by

doing that, I was already listening to my instincts as a designer. When I make things with my hands, when I give them form and shape and even invent a new technique as I fold and manipulate cloth, I am designing. I have everything in my head, and then I feel, feel, feel my way through a new creation.

By the end of high school, I was creating kitelike shapes that resembled a three-dimensional version of the flat paper patterns I had first learned how to use in elementary school. The ability to use clothing as communication, combined with the language of music and dance, opened up the whole world for me, because I learned to see shapes in fluid motion. This would influence my design sensibility forever. I was simply doing what came naturally, practicing the important social skill of expressing and sharing my vision while adding to the new culture blossoming all around me.

FALLING IN LOVE WITH ART

I wasn't a bad student in high school. Quite the opposite: I made a point of sitting in the front row of my classrooms, paying close attention, and absorbing every last drop of knowledge my teachers had to offer. However, school seemed less pertinent now that I was so eagerly attuned to learning from the world beyond the classroom. I had no time to waste in school because I could sense that the world was waiting.

One exception to this was my high school art class. I enjoyed all aspects of my art class. I began to paint complete paintings with tempera paints on writing paper and glue them over the printed wallpaper of my bedroom. My walls became a patchwork of images, art over more art, not a peaceful visual environment.

For one birthday, a friend of the family gave me a set of oil paints and prestretched canvases. I again felt the rush of excitement that I always felt in the presence of professional tools. My mother received the monthly Spanish-language magazine, *Vanidades*, which ran a page each month with a photograph of a famous oil painting by the Masters. Gradually, I painted those famous paintings to teach myself technique. I didn't paint the entire work. Instead, I dissected and abstracted the work by painting only different sections of the masterpieces that most interested me.

Just as I had always loved taking apart toys and machines and putting them back together again to see how they were made, I now sought to discover and understand the distinct individual components that made up the whole of each famous painting. I studied a lot of sections from the paintings Picasso had done during his Blue Period, for instance, because I wanted to work in a space I was able to control.

It was in my Spanish class, freshman year of high school, that I first met Ruben, the young man who would later become the love of my life and who still makes me tick twenty-seven married years later. We were also in art class

together. Despite the fact that our families lived in the same
neighborhood, just ten blocks apart, we had never met before
high school because we went to different elementary schools.
In addition, whereas my parents were a sociable couple
who went out often and knew everyone in the area, Ruben's
parents were more conservative and preferred to stay home.

Ruben always tells me how he fell in love with me at first
sight within seconds, despite the fact that, with my short hair
and plucked eyebrows, I looked more like a thirty-year-old
divorcee than a high school freshman. He says that he also
noticed my clothes, because I was dressed from head to toe
in my own original work. He was convinced from the first
moment we met that I would one day become his wife.

I had no such premonition, and so I wasn't open to his
innuendos. I knew only that Ruben was easy to talk to in class
and had a very dark sense of humor. He was very shy and
quiet, but with a certain presence. He was skinny and wore
braces. This made him seem too young to be interesting to me
at the time, since I had long been in the habit of going out with
my older sisters and their friends.

Meanwhile, Ruben and I got along so well as friends
that we even began collaborating on projects. Our very first
collaboration was on a poster that I was making in art class. I'd
painted a cold-looking ocean in misty greens and blues with

rough waves, and I wanted to add a boat. I could do color, but I couldn't put a line down to save my life.

"Do you think you could draw a boat on this for me?" I asked Ruben.

"Of course," he said, and he did it in such an unusual way, from a very close perspective, half in and half out of the water, that I loved that poster and admired his talent as an artist even more.

Like me, Ruben had begun to voice his passions through his art and with his hands. I trusted him immediately because his hands made such gifts, his pencils and paints creating beauty, color and humor before my very eyes. It was like magic.

Whether I was making a dress or Ruben was drawing a boat, we had both seen in ourselves, and in each other, that your creativity is your voice. It deserves to be sung often and at the top of your lungs.

Part 2

love ......

4 Entering a Love State of Mind

The hardest things to own in life are time and love.

TIME IS THE ULTIMATE AND MOST

essential ingredient for a life well lived. It's

important to learn how to weave time into

your solutions, whether you're solving a

design dilemma or a relationship problem.

Take many deep breaths in a day, and your

body and soul will be the richer for it. How did I fall in love? I took a deep breath and let it in. It was all around, patiently waiting for me.

Whether you're building a bridge, creating a sculpture, designing a pair of trousers, or making love work, if you want to make something of quality, it's essential to pay attention to detail because it is woven by time. After high school, I took a self-imposed sabbatical and removed myself from the automatic treadmill of life. I gave myself permission to fine-tune the most important detail of my own life: the formation of me.

I think that during the first part of our lives, we are being formed. Then, at the legal age of eighteen, you have the right and the responsibility to begin informing your life, zeroing in on who you are and on what you are going to become. By taking time, I discovered that it is useless to be a slave to the clock. Time will be on your side if you are true to your own tempo.

MY INDEPENDENCE DAY

High school graduation is the first important fork in the road that you will encounter in life, because from then on, things will start changing, and change will be happening to you. To this day, I think of graduation day—anybody's graduation day from anything—as a personal independence day. This is when you should enter that delicious state of mind where you feel free to go with your own flow and are calm enough to follow your inner clock. It's almost like a sacred ceremonial space and a place inside you reserved for certain times in your life.

From my point of view, to graduate from high school is to finally earn a certain independence—you get to be the one to decide which way you should go next, which turn on the road

you will take. You have been preparing yourself to this point
with the tools that will give you the freedom and foundation
to think for yourself. You get to add your learned academic
knowledge and accumulated life lessons to your own natural
instincts and intuition, mixing the lessons everyone else has
taught you with your natural attributes and gifts.

What did I do after my own high school graduation?
Nothing! Nothing my heart was not open to. I am forever
grateful to my brave and patient parents for giving me this
gift of time. This detour from the rhythms of life up until then
allowed me a necessary exercise for reflection. It will be for most
of us the last time for a long time that time will be on our side.

I welcomed high school graduation and my new liberty
with open arms. I flirted with this free and rewarding feeling of
nothingness. No schedules, no pressures: Just my mind, armed
with the basic tools to move forward and better understand
where I was headed. I had achieved, for now, the freedom to
think for myself and to act on my thoughts while discovering
the openness of my heart. Finishing high school was a clear goal
to owning my independence. After spending so many years
learning and absorbing all of society's rules, I found it almost a
mandate to throw the rule book up in the air, dissect it, question it,
reshuffle it, and start to reapply it to myself and develop a deeper
personal understanding. My curiosity and determination to enter

adulthood with my own spectacles and look at the future from my particular vantage point was the unstructured time my parents must have thought could prepare me for a happy and fruitful life.

STANDING STILL AND LOSING MYSELF

As I was leaving adolescence behind and entering the pure definition of what it means to become an adult, I was slapped with the realization of going from carefree to "now what?" It was a confusing time. While some of my friends were headed to college, others were increasingly busy "losing" themselves. I had already experienced personal growth and control with my sewing hobby, and I had gained the trust of my parents necessary for them to give me some slack. I had also gotten a fair grip on the monstrous adolescent insecurities that might have otherwise gotten in the way of a healthy perspective on future opportunities. Yet, this was the first time that my life took such uncontrollable leaps forward, backward, sideways, you name it. My emotions were attacking me from every which way and needed to be processed at a very fast pace.

I trusted my instincts, even if I didn't have a clue what I wanted to do. I physically stepped on the brakes—a great metaphor for wanting to "stop time." I wanted to travel inward, not outward, and I realized that the only way I could do this was to take the time to stand still. I had always been an active person, so this wasn't easy. The difficulty of this exercise made me realize that it was an even more important step in the development of who I was, because it would set the stage for who I might become.

After high school there is a time of physical and mental growth, and the most typical reaction is to try to move ahead, sometimes literally moving away to experience a new world and surroundings. But my compass pointed me in a different direction. I went searching for a deeper meaning that went beyond the things that were already surrounding me. From the obvious and familiar, I set out to discover my inner world.

I let time pass me by, and took from this period what suited me and felt right. I had come to the conclusion that there are at least two directions that you can take for personal growth: inward and outward. You can run after new places and experiences, a choice that may lead you to a treasure chest full of novelties and new adventures. Or, you can activate your inner clock, and absorb content from your own unique universe. Depending on where you are in life, you can choose which of these travels better suits your purpose. I chose the latter. This state of mind allowed me to fall in love with my interests and with the world, inspiring me to try to live up to my own expectations.

When I say that "I took the time," I must admit that the time was there for the taking. I will be forever grateful to my parents for giving me this space, for lodging and feeding me during what I like to call my "free-range time." They did not pressure me to make a career choice. They bravely, if nervously, stood by and waited for me to ask to be gently watered like a tree, and they watched me for any signs of blooming.

It was during this quiet time that I fell deeply in love with Ruben. In this selfish space, I understood how to share the best of myself, because I learned how to fall in love with everything that had given meaning to my life.

ROAD MAP TO FREEDOM

What I discovered during that enriching period of my life is that I value having the time to think and the independence to act in ways that might seem inconvenient with the way most of the world operates. This is still true today. I avoid meaningless schedules whenever possible. The object of the game is to give your very best whenever possible to any given situation, project, or person you choose.

For me, time is anything but a clock.
It is not a numerical experience. Time is
held and captured in the things around
me. Time is the accumulation of my
experiences, and love is often the reward.
When I think of time as a shape, I think of it as a circle
inside a square. With patience, you can focus on
your goals and mold that square into a circle, or stretch a circle
into a square. The gift of focus means that you have the power to
shape your own future.

As I began to discover during that first year after high school,
stopping to take a deep breath is the first step you can take in
combining your surroundings and your memories to arrive at
the meaning of your whole experience. I see time as the ultimate
luxury. It is also the most essential ingredient for a life well lived.

The idea of losing yourself seemed to me to be a waste of
very valuable time. You have already spent years cultivating
and becoming who you are. "Losing yourself" signifies an
undoing, an unmaking of yourself instead of building,
forming, or sculpting yourself. Having to "lose yourself"
implies having to start from scratch, when in fact the
accumulation of your experiences is what gives you
the resources you need to move forward and better
understand the direction you'd like to go in next.

Your experiences are like the wedge under the foot of a sprinter at the moment that runner hears, "On your mark, get set, go!" Good or bad, that wedge of experiences is solid and tangible, and those experiences are the very things that can push you ahead.

If you must lose yourself to find yourself, this is best done when you disconnect from the structured time imposed by the preset social countdown and take stock of the things within you that simply make you feel whole. For me, that meant sewing, gardening, and contemplating nature and space—or doing any other physical activity, as long as I didn't have to join the automatic treadmill of a prestructured life.

WHAT MOST PEOPLE DON'T REALIZE is that time really is on your side if you stop watching the clock. You are rewarded by time itself. And this sense of freedom from structured time is essential to me. In order to bloom into your full potential, you have to allow yourself this free-range time, a time when you are not yet sure where you are going but are certain to arrive exactly at your absolute and proper destination. This state of mind allows you to fall in love with your interests, with your surroundings, and with your world, inspiring you to make a difference by adding the very best part of yourself to the tapestry of life.

My love of freedom and the luxury of time are elements that I try to infuse into my clothes. When you take the time to care, to focus on whatever you are doing, this sense of focus and dedication will be infused into your work, no matter what your work may be. People can really feel this. I certainly can feel it in other people's work.

This is what communication through art and design is all about for me: Not how fast or how many you can make, but how deep or how pertinent, how enduring and resonating the contact is with the artwork. That is why the idea of scheduled fashion shows doesn't hold my attention for long. I would rather have fashion shows all year round and celebrate design on my own schedule, when my work has reached its prime-time bloom. This free-range schedule allows me to create more genuine intimacy with my clothes and clients.

This sense of timelessness is something that I adore, and the way I personally like to dress. I put this timelessness into my designs. To create something that can stand the test of time and has its own soul is always one of my design goals. This point of view can be at odds with the idea of fashion itself, but to achieve a design that is free of an expiration date gives me personal and professional satisfaction.

What gave me the confidence to always create according to my own rules and my own schedule? I don't think I could have done it any other way, but for me, confidence is born out of self-respect. I address all changes in my life from the very dependable core of my character, which I believe is the meaning of self-respect. It can be difficult to fake confidence, but self-respect is a basic ingredient that we can all live up to, and from there, confidence is born.

During this important hiatus after high school, I began to nourish self-respect and self-knowledge. Since then, I have always addressed every challenge in my life from the core of self-respect. The idea of getting something "right" or having the right answer becomes relative and completely defined by your own standards.

You can arrive at your own right answers only through experience and time, as you test out what you don't already know or understand. I take great pleasure in the experience of not knowing. It gives me the abundance of energy I need to figure things out and think my way through new and challenging ideas. These are the unexpected ingredients outside of myself that refresh and nourish my pool of knowledge, and help open up unexpected avenues of thought. These moments of not knowing are valuable, and often lead to great opportunities, as I explore and invent new solutions.

As I began to discover, in opening up my life and heart after high school, the unexpected happenings are often the events that lead you into new territories and discoveries. That's still true in my career today. I try to maintain a very open mind. I have great respect for people who have accumulated knowledge through their studies; a well-read person can use society's recorded lessons to form and improve a new society. By the same token, I am inspired by individuals who take the time to observe, absorb, and reflect upon their own lives, their personal surroundings, and society as a whole, and walk away with deeper self-understanding.

THE LUSH REWARDS OF INVESTING TIME IN YOURSELF AND YOUR IDEAS

Giving yourself the freedom to follow your instincts means that you must be generous with your own time. Allowing yourself the time you need to follow your own hunches is the way to achieve and discover who you are, and how best to design and create things that truly reflect your individuality. Some of my favorite design breakthroughs have been in development in my studio for months, or even years, before I send them off to market.

For instance, it took me many years of trial and error to develop and refine my gusset sleeves until I was happy with their performance and how they affected the look of a garment's

silhouette. As I perfected the sleeve, I ended up
creating a trail of other designs.

Certain patterns, like the
one for the burlap beach
bag I first sold at Fiorucci in 1984, later
morphed into different concepts as I experimented
with evolving these shapes into sleeves, skirts,
dresses, and capes. Without the generous time to
explore and perfect concepts, fashion designers would
randomly reintroduce and reshuffle empty looks and
merchandise without rhyme or reason, and fashion
design wouldn't be able to claim its place as an art form.
Spending time on the things you love and that
are important to you defines not only your
work, but your personality as well. If
you love growing things in the soil, that
love clearly shows in your garden, which
will reward you by gushing luscious
blooms. These same lush rewards will show
in your work and other endeavors sooner or
later, no matter what you're doing, provided you put
in the effort. You can make no better investment than
spending time with your own ideas. Your generosity in
granting time to yourself will be well rewarded.

Doing this on your own time and by yourself is paramount to learning how to follow your own instincts and discovering your originality. Anything new, whether it's a dress, a song, or a painting, will not be easily understood right away— sometimes not even by yourself, the creator. You have to feel free to be misunderstood and allow time to work its magic.

The magic of time often permits you to connect the
dots, and for the rest of the world to get comfortable
with new ideas. Creating in an atmosphere conducive to
experimentation and open to exploring any ideas that come
to you, even those that seem contrary or contradictory, is
essential to me. I try to surround myself, my workplace,
and even my life with this feeling. I could not express a new
thought, come up with new color combinations, or play
with textures if I didn't give myself that creative freedom to
constantly try new things.

That, for me, is the essence, the whole point of why we
make new designs and have fashion shows: not necessarily
to show what is correct, or to try to hit on the right answer,
but to suggest new ideas we have discovered. In fashion, all
the wrong is one day right. Women themselves will get to
make the decisions about what will become fashion trends by
choosing the ideas they can use, and adopting those ideas into
their lives. We women decide what is fashion, no matter what
we are told. This is the most empowering aspect of fashion: We
activate it into actual use, and make the fantasy a reality.

When I work with young students today, these are all key
lessons that I try to impart. I want them to realize that, in order
to create a different design landscape, it's a great exercise to
stop consuming as a spectator. Instead, they can travel deep

within themselves to develop their own interior dialogues and points of view, so that they can reach their potential as makers.

THAT FIRST SUMMER AFTER HIGH school seemed to last a century. Time passed at a leisurely, lovely snail's pace. I cultivated my flower box garden with a new appreciation and infinite attention to everything from weeding and fertilizing to pruning plants. I grew geraniums of giant, prehistoric sizes and brilliant colors.

This was the first time that I discovered I had a really green thumb. Ruben jokes now that I can only grow specimens, saying that I am incapable of keeping any plant from growing nine feet tall, or even taller, if the ceiling allows! Gardening did expose me to patience. Growth takes time, and while I anticipated the beautiful blossoms, I found myself enjoying the process of gardening. I learned to appreciate the fact that not even plants are at their peak at all times, and that each stage of growth has its own beauty and unique form.

My parents had observed me making my clothes, and they were always supportive of my diligence and interest in my craft. My father, at this time, asked me to help out a friend who owned a bridal shop. He didn't imagine that I'd earn a living making clothes—nobody did, least of all me—but he knew that I liked to sew, and his friend needed help.

It was a disaster. For the first time, I experienced a tremendous pressure in my life, working at that bridal shop. The owner would cut the dresses and I'd sew them on the machine, while other women did the handwork with beads and sequins and buttons. I never made it out to the front of the store, because I was working in the back room. Watching my father's friend deal with the bridezillas was so terrifying that I didn't even let the poor woman pay me, for fear that I might get caught up in the business and have to return!

Meanwhile, my father's textile mill had moved to Atlanta. He didn't want to move with them from New Jersey, so he began working with a friend who owned a wholesale and retail clothing store in Union City. My father eventually bought the store, and asked me to help him create the window displays, which I did happily each week.

I learned a lot about creating good feng shui through designing those windows to attract his clientele. This was during the birth of the designer jeans craze, and for one particular window, I improvised a wash day scene, complete with an old metal tub, scrubbing board, and clothesline. On the line I hung Calvin Klein, Gloria Vanderbilt, and Jordache jeans.

Otherwise, I was free to pursue my ideas, thoughts, and self-appointed projects on my own time. I continued to make clothing at home. Sewing was still my biggest passion, and

I felt even more joy in my craft now that I had more time to spend perfecting it. I especially loved experimenting and challenging myself with different fabrics. In a lot of ways, I suppose that finding the right design and fabric made me feel the way a scientist must when discovering something new in a laboratory after months of experimentation: It's pure bliss when you have a breakthrough discovery moment.

I used every moment of this free-range sabbatical of the soul to experiment. The more I learned about making clothes, the more I wanted to learn. I never once thought about turning this passion into a profession. However, without even knowing it, I was opening myself up to the overwhelming power of self-expression through fashion design by constantly feeding my passion for sewing and deliberately making the time and space in my life to follow my artistic interests.

The advice I give to young artists today is that you must love what you are doing, because with love and focus, you will become successful. Give yourself the luxury of time to focus on yourself and cultivate your mind. You certainly do not want to be caged into doing something you do not fully love for the rest of your life. You must envision the bigger picture, then focus in on the details to arrive at your own original idea. That is dedication to detail, where you are the detail. This is an important life credo, one that is constant in everything I make.

I weave this into my garments, making clothing with such great care that, if the wearer looks closely enough, she will experience the same quality of time and attention to detail that I brought to making them.

ENTER FRIENDS, EXIT LOVERS

Ruben, the shy boy I had met in high school, had become a very good friend of mine through the years, and was starting to grow into himself. Slowly but surely, he was sprouting and sparking ideas that were starting to captivate me creatively and intellectually, if not romantically yet. Life is funny that way, but as Ruben has remarked regarding our own personal love story, "Women often enter love through the doorway of friendship."

Ruben and his family had come to the U.S. from Cuba just a year before we arrived. He grew up at the extreme tail end of West New York, so we never crossed paths until we met in high school. He was my complete opposite, in that he wasn't very social and was a bit of a loner, which is what I liked about him instantly.

Ruben had taken a photography class in his junior year of high school and had asked me to pose for some pictures for class. He took black-and-white photos of me, which he hand-colored with vegetable dyes and food coloring. They were horrifically interesting, dark but with a sense of humor. They looked like they could have been film stills from a Technicolor musical horror movie—a very Toledo point of view to this day. I was touched that he asked me to pose since I was pretty shy and also because I totally trusted him creatively.

Those pictures started Ruben's art career when he was still in high school, and I am happy to know that I was part of his dive into real life. While in high school, we all took a school trip to the Museum of Modern Art as part of an art class. Some of us got lost and ended up at a shop called Fiorucci by mistake. It was pouring rain, and to get out from the soaking wet, a few of us stumbled into the shop.

Fiorucci was the daytime headquarters of Studio 54. The music, the people, the scene, and the atmosphere were still at their peak in 1978–79. It was there, at Fiorucci on that wet day, that we met our friend for life, Joey Arias, whom I inspiringly call my midnight poet. Joey has been the unofficial cultural mayor of Manhattan ever since he arrived by car from California with Kim Hastreiter, founder of *Paper* magazine and a cultural guru herself. When we walked in, Joey snatched the cheap black vinyl portfolio held together with duct tape and rubber bands that Ruben was carrying under his arm and proceeded to look inside. There, he came across the pictures of me that Ruben had hand-painted and cut into oddly shaped, jagged boxes.

Joey loved them instantly, and took them and Ruben over to the woman who ran the postcard concession stand at Fiorucci. Her name was Sweet B, and her kiosk was in the middle of the store. She sold postcards by different artists and photographers there, some famous, some not. Sweet B also fell in love with the pictures, and ordered two or three dozen of each image.

Ruben was thrilled to have made his first art sale, and excited to be earning some much needed cash. He had always worked as a kid since he was nine or ten, selling newspapers and doing the usual kid stuff. Off he went to his high school photo class, where he proceeded to print, hand-color, and sign his postcards. He delivered them to Fiorucci once or twice a month. It was a very encouraging start for a young artist.

It was here at Fiorucci that Ruben first met Andy Warhol through Joey, as well as Keith Haring and Kenny Scharf, who were just starting to become well-known artists themselves and who were starting to collaborate with Andy. Fiorucci was the central meeting ground for artists, designers, models, actors, and writers: You name them, and they were there. Everyone crossed paths. Places like Fiorucci can happen only organically, and come along once a decade, if you're lucky.

I say "lucky" because these retail places happen to catch and define the spirit of the moment, just like that hair salon I had first gone to in the Village ten years before. Like that salon, Fiorucci was part museum, gallery, clubhouse, bar, social club, and cabaret. If you're lucky enough to know a place like this, you can really get a great cultural education that is years ahead of where society is headed next.

Fiorucci was also a marvelously democratic sort of place. Where else in the world could two Cuban immigrant teenagers casually meet Halston, Lena Horne, and Kay Thompson? Ruben also met Klaus Nomi at Fiorucci, and eventually joined his band, or rather, his performance group.

Klaus was a multitalented artist and performer. He was also one of the very best bakers in town, making Black Forest cakes in his living room–kitchen for top-notch restaurants in order to make a living before he became well known for his operatic New Wave performances.

Klaus and Joey performed together, and were at the epicenter of a whole new wave of art and performance culture that really solidified what became known as the Downtown scene. They helped set the tone for what made New York City so special and alive in the

late 1970s and early 1980s. The memorable appearance of
Joey and Klaus singing backup for David Bowie on *Saturday
Night Live* in 1979 was a coming of age for that whole era—
Downtown went national on that very night.

. . .

RUBEN EVENTUALLY ENROLLED AT THE School of Visual Arts after graduating from high school. He always says that he was there "for five minutes," but really it was more like ten. He attended just one semester, yet we didn't finish paying the student loan until many years after we were married.

Knowing that he loved art, Ruben really wanted to learn how to paint like the Old Masters. His goal was to learn how to mix pigments and make his own varnishes. He loved to draw more than anything else, and was already a good draftsman. He took painting courses only so he could finally work with canvases and paints.

Ruben was disappointed to find out that there were no more Old Masters teaching at the School of Visual Arts that semester. Instead, his teachers were more about exposing students to "conceptual" things, like painting with sugar and mixing glitter into paint. Since Ruben had already painted with food dyes and supermarket finds because that was all he could afford, he quickly realized that maybe going to art school was not a great idea for him. It was too expensive, especially because purchasing the art supplies he needed was way out of his ballpark.

Besides the financial difficulties, Ruben had gotten a bit of advice from Andy Warhol, who told him to quit school. "Just do what you do already, but bigger, and you'll be fine," Andy said. So Ruben did just that and never looked back.

After high school graduation, I stopped seeing Ruben as often. It is curious that, when a piece of a pattern in your life suddenly goes missing, every other piece comes undone.

CUPID WORKS IN MYSTERIOUS WAYS. Ruben knew, from the moment he first saw me in that freshman high school Spanish class, that I would be his wife one day. For me, though, that potent chemical attraction happened several years later, when I was nineteen years old. Partly, I think it happened because I was finally open to the idea of falling in love. In that summer after high school, I'd had time to reflect and experiment with my creative designs, nurturing the artist within. Now I was ready to look outward toward the rest of my life.

I became aware that my nightlife had lost its sparkle unless Ruben was part of the gang. He had been my constant friend and collaborator in art, and I couldn't believe that I was falling in love. After four years of knowing him, it took one summer without him to fall in love. It's as if suddenly something in me woke up! I became newly aware of Ruben as a man, physically as well as emotionally. I like to say that he had now grown up, but in fact, I think it was me who was doing the growing.

I set out to reclaim him, using everything in my power to put myself back into his life. As Ruben drifted into his own life in the city, I made a point at this time to lure him back to me. It's a funny thing, how timing and love can sometimes need realignment. Being with Ruben was the obvious sign of happiness in my path, yet I had not seen it. True to my character, I don't always see clearly, but feel my way to the right place and time. I am relieved to say that it was definitely not meant to be puppy love.

Fortunately for me, Ruben delighted in my artistic expression, just as much as I admired his drawing and painting. We loved in each other the magic of wonder, and to this day, we keep that ingredient of discovery alive. There is no truer fact than that you never really know the person you are with. But, better than knowing is having confidence in not knowing.

During this time, I continued gardening, growing flowers to monstrous proportions. Ruben loved my green thumb, which he said put him in awe while at the same time made him feel peaceful. I continued sewing and developing ideas about clothing construction, and my nighttime social scene changed to daylight. All I could see was that love was in the air.

We constantly went away with groups of friends on weekends, or even for weeklong excursions. We hiked up and down more mountains than I can remember and took bicycle trips through Pennsylvania Dutch country, staying in youth hostels and experiencing the wonderful Amish food—I've never tasted anything as delicious as that homemade butter. We also rented beach houses on the Jersey shore.

That summer, Ruben and I found every excuse to explore the change from adolescence to adulthood, and I took every opportunity to remind Ruben that he was in love with me. I knew that summer that I had to lure him or lose him forever.

In life and in love, there are always those fork-in-the-road moments that you can feel deep inside. Sometimes it's an obvious sign; sometimes it's a subtle shift in the direction of the wind. But it can suddenly appear as clear as a stop sign. This is when your body, mind and spirit all seem to jump into action to save you, or at least to point you in the right direction. With time, you learn to trust this instinct. In fact, you can't ignore it. And with time, love can either grow stronger, fuse, and strengthen, or grow apart until it breaks. I focused my compass on what gave me joy, and I ultimately learned that a key ingredient to my happiness was Ruben.

5 Nurturing a Love of Art

Never be afraid of the unknown. It is the act

of creating, not the result, that is the most

exhilarating, refreshing, and deeply satisfying

journey of discovery.

THERE IS TREMENDOUS POWER

in untamed self-expression, because it opens

you up to finding your own path and true

calling in life. I learned this by trusting myself

and realizing that it was important not to

be afraid of the unknown. I deliberately sidestepped the prepaved paths of work and school in order to nurture my love of art.

In doing so, I discovered that there was a great freedom in looking within myself to map out my own journey according to an internal compass.

ART WITHOUT AN AGENDA

With no particular agenda in mind after high school, I signed up for night classes at both Parsons (The New School for Design) and The Fashion Institute of Technology (FIT). I was not yet charting out any professional career path. I was simply investigating more deeply some topics of interest I sensed I needed to learn more about. I approached the two schools with different expectations.

Parsons represented a more roundabout artistic approach to a possible fashion career for me, and also allowed me to explore more diverse fields of investigation. I focused on taking classes with a slant toward art, yet in an environment infused with fashion. My classes consisted mostly of life drawing, ceramics, and pottery.

I see art as having no preset boundaries, and because of this, it is where I feel most comfortable. Creativity stalks every profession. It is just waiting to happen. If you are going to become really good at something, you will be innovative and discover your own path. By allowing myself to roam in and out of my areas of interest, I was connecting the dots toward where I would eventually end up. I took courses that I sensed would offer me different perspectives. Some were love at first sight. Others, not so much.

I especially adored making pottery and throwing pots on the wheel, which I quickly learned to handle. There was something extremely satisfying about working out the object you were forming from every direction. My ceramic projects became more and more ambitious, with each week's lesson reaching a point where my instructors asked me to please not work on such a large scale. The seashell formations I was exploring were taking up all of the space in the kilns during firing, so much that no other students could fit their work inside it!

I ended up coming in on weekends to use the kiln, because I didn't want to give up making these huge, pleasing shapes. I had to enlist help, though, because I did need extra pairs of hands to get my giant ceramic barnacles in and out of the kilns. I didn't mind. I was working on instinct. I loved these nature-inspired, airy, handcrafted shapes. These pots were a precursor to some of the organically geometric shapes in my later fashion collections, though of course I wasn't thinking that way at the time. And that is the wonderful surprise about education: It exposes you to new things, and leads you to your next cycle of learning.

I also took a sculpture class, a costume design course, and a Japanese language class at Parsons as part of my "follow your instincts" movement. I was being guided by my natural curiosities and interests and not any particular career path. My quest for knowledge and the broadening of my interests would eventually lead me to my future, but it would have been unnatural for me to say, "I want to be a fashion designer." I had to arrive at that conclusion organically, through the acts of doing and loving.

Another practice I loved immediately was life drawing. The abstraction of the human body, with all of its planes and intersecting, movable boundaries, has always intrigued and amazed me. There are so many different ways to interpret the human form. Although we haven't changed as a species or evolved in any significant manner, like growing an extra head or appendages that would require new forms of tailoring, human anatomy is a fountain of inspiration for me as a designer.

The variations of movement, and all the parts that sum up the human body— it's muscles and tissues and the skeleton— are the essence of great designs. I fixate on parts of the body in order to form a new silhouette, whether I choose the more traditional fashion "acupuncture points"—as I like to call the waist, the neckline, and the cleavage—or how I focus in on an armpit, all are valid when a dialogue with body and cloth takes place. I find it most inspiring to approach draping a body from the bottom up, against gravity.

I was drawn to study costume design at Parsons because I was always fascinated by the psychology of clothing. The reasons people pick certain articles of clothing to wear, and what those choices say about them, whether they are aware of it or not. Choices in color, texture, materials, and the cut of our clothes can all add up to a composite portrait of our inner psychological makeup—our hidden dreams, desires, and motivations.

The merger of literature and the visual arts is summed up best for me by costume

design. Any ideas that can be summed up in words and paragraphs can also be said through clothing. The art of visual presentation and styling is living proof that fashion is a form of language itself, and a very potent tool for communication. One obvious pop example of this is how we choose to wear words on our T-shirts.

I tackled my school costume design projects with much gusto, conceptualizing productions for ballets and plays. But, for all of my sincere efforts, my teachers agreed that I would never make it as a costume designer, because the costumes themselves would have been active participants in the performance. They were completely correct.

Dressing a character in a story is incredibly challenging. A great costume designer is aware of the parameters that are constantly driving the performance. This is totally different from creating fashion without references. My friend Dr. Deborah Nadoolman, who was president of the Costume Designer's Guild for many years, has written extensively on this subject. She has designed costumes as varied as the fedora and jacket worn by Indiana Jones and the red jacket Michael Jackson wore in the "Thriller" music video. Deborah believes that the character dictates every nuance, and costume design must serve the final purpose of letting the characters play their parts and advance the story.

I appreciate a theatrical performance for being just that:

theatrical. The idea that theater is not an imitation of life, but an altered version of reality where poetic freedom, a heightened awareness of symbols, and visual equations are not only encouraged but essential in telling a story, is what I find so satisfying about witnessing a live performance. The willingness of the audience to suspend reality and join in participating in a fantastic journey is still a magical experience for me whenever I go to the theater or watch a movie. Fashion is a very important part of this whole equation. While I really did enjoy theatrical costume design, I was most intrigued by participating in the dressing of the society that the stories would later be written about. The expression of fashion, the unscripted seasonal parade of clothing, changing nonstop like the seasons, year after year.

This realization led me to focus on my dressmaking and tailoring techniques by attending classes at FIT. When I told my father what I wanted to do, he surprised me by coming home from work one day and presenting me with an enormous leather portfolio. To my father, remember, the world was full of useful tools, and he saw this as one of mine: a gorgeous portfolio in cordovan leather with a great zipper on the outside. I still have that portfolio.

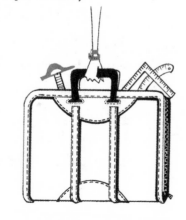

What inspired my father to make such a lavish purchase? I still wonder. I suppose that he must have been watching me throughout my mini-sabbatical, and wondering what I was going to do and what direction I'd finally choose for my future. He had always been supportive of my sewing. Now he was pleased to see me headed in that direction—or probably glad that I was going back to school for anything at all, I imagine.

At any rate, having that beautiful gift inspired me, because it made me feel as if I should get to work and make something worthy of such a grand portfolio. My father's gesture, and having the portfolio in my hand, propelled me to focus, stop floating, and become a professional.

CHOOSING TO ATTEND COURSES AT FIT was a way for me to start focusing on the fashion industry as a territory for exploration. I had realized by then that my heart was in the pure expression of fashion design. At FIT, I was now surrounded by tools of the trade that I never knew existed. I was also exposed to the technical knowledge of my instructors and fellow students—knowledge that, until this point, had been a missing link in my fashion education. Until now, I had been mostly self-taught; I was finally ready to learn the rules and steps for draping on a dressmaker's dummy, how to use

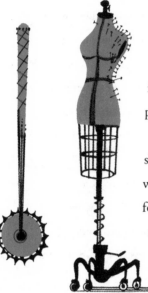

proper tools to transfer cloth ideas to paper, and how to go about marking the grains so as not to fall off the weave in a cloth—all missing parts of the puzzle up to this point.

I also learned to make my own slopers—custom-fitted basic patterns, which can then be used to make patterns for many different styles using particular measurements. Using slopers helped me create the classics within my own design vocabulary because I was able to return to a previous idea again and again to perfect it. I was fine while free to make an abstract dress come to life on my own. But, in order to try my hand at making anything classic and tailored, I knew that I would have to master the more technical and traditional aspects of sewing, including drafting patterns. I was also eager to crack the mystery of grading patterns to make the same design in different sizes.

The most brilliant aspect of taking evening classes at FIT was that I was surrounded by adult professionals who were all working in the industry by day. These were all serious students who made perfect classmates, because we were all on a mission

of self-improvement. There was no wasting time for these folks. They were there to perfect and polish their skills, with hopes of upgrading their professional abilities. Some were pattern makers who wanted to better grasp the sensitivity and secrets of draping. Others were seamstresses who wanted to graduate to pattern making because the pay is much better. Through working with them in my classes, I was able to absorb the fashion culture through the reality of their day-to-day experiences working in the fashion industry.

Becoming a master of fashion design takes great discipline for the art of making clothes and a Zen-like commitment to your vision. Because I was self-taught, I made things according to my own ideas, rules, and techniques. In the beginning, doing things your own way is always the best way to conceptualize the raw ideas that will later become the source of your

body of work, and eventually your fingerprint on the world and your identity as a designer in a very competitive field. This isn't the easiest thing to achieve, but if you can do it, you can become financially successful in the industry.

For me, the best reward for having started out making things my own way is that, whenever a pattern maker declares that something can't be done, I feel confident and free enough to tackle any design approach by doing it myself. Once the concept is realized, it can then be perfected by the pattern makers.

However, through my classes at FIT, now I was deliberately taking the steps I needed to possibly enter the fashion field. Doing things my own way until then helped me develop my own vision and ideas. Now, becoming familiar with the way the fashion industry makes clothes and exposing myself to the basic ingredients of the trade, I gained the skills and confidence I needed to dive even more deeply into my design ideas, as well as the sophisticated knowledge I needed to boost into my explorations. Combining my intuitive, self-taught approach with the industry's standard rules of construction gave me a more solid foundation from which I could enter uncharted territory and approach the draping process from my own point of view.

For instance, I could already create kitelike dresses in amorphous shapes, because I knew how to make the fabric hang in certain abstract ways. I knew that different fabrics made me feel different emotions, and that I had a special connection to cloth that was visceral rather than visual. Sometimes, I looked at a certain fabric and knew that I wanted to build with it and mold it into a particular shape. Other times, I'd study a fabric and its relationship to gravity, and think about wanting to deconstruct that cloth in ways that would let a garment flow down my body like rippling water.

However, for me to make clothing that looked structured as well as draped, I needed to learn more and extend my level of expertise. Tailoring was my holy grail. Tailoring was a parallel universe to all that I had taught myself by draping fabric on my own body. In my own School of the Self-Taught, motion, drape, and movement were the primary ingredients.

Now, in Tailoring Class at FIT, I learned about precision, symmetry, and balance. I was determined to learn how to create fitted necklines and how to set sleeves traditionally— basic rules that I had never learned. I knew that the shared language of the fashion industry would allow me to better communicate and execute my design ideas.

For many students, this "cabinet of curiosities" approach to learning that I experienced is often the first step toward your eventual fine-tuning. You should be free to dabble in and investigate everything that interests you, especially while you're in school. Through naturally weaving together your true interests, you won't have to search for a career. Your career will find *you*.

Start with your own point of view and self-taught, intuitive ideas, and then you can layer on the proper, tried-and-true lessons. My night courses at FIT and Parsons gave me the knowledge and skills I needed to fully control how I expressed my emotions and thoughts through fashion design.

MAGIC AT THE MET

In couture, what makes a dress extraordinary is rooted at its very core. An exceptional design starts from its epicenter. Clothing is transformed into art when it is so well crafted and perfectly engineered that it functions as one with the wearer and expresses the vision of the maker.

As I took my classes at FIT, I became more technically proficient as a designer and polished my seamstress skills. I wasn't concentrating on the outside of my clothing—on how it *looked*—because good style was already a given for me. Instead, I really focused on their insides. I became ever more obsessed with the construction and the performance of my creations, challenging myself with the goal of perfecting my concepts to go beyond just being a good-looking idea. The patterns had to really work well in motion, which meant that the architecture of the garments had to be sound and honest in its design.

The crucial part of my DNA as a designer and my work as a seamstress is to understand the "make," or, in other words, the construction of a garment.

Whenever I'm about to start to work on a new design, I always ask myself these questions:

Is this a new idea?

Does it do its job well?

Is it a durable design idea?

And, perhaps most important of all: Does this garment enhance the wearer and make her feel both protected and empowered?

For me, fashion approaches fine art when all of these elements work seamlessly. A really great design is like a great composition, in that all of the notes in the melody and harmony have to be played well. In the hands of a great conductor and the best musicians, even an ordinary composition can go from good to great, and from great to extraordinary. In couture, extraordinary is where you want to end up.

The place where I first completely absorbed this key lesson—and where it became clear to me that fashion design is, indeed, an art form—was The Costume Institute of the Metropolitan Museum of Art. In 1979, when I was not quite twenty years old, Ruben introduced me to one of his friends who was interning at

the Met's Costume Institute. She knew that I could sew because
of Ruben's many stories about me, so she took me along to the
Met to meet Richard, the person in charge of accepting interns.
Richard helped organize the interns and volunteer workforce
during the preparation of large exhibitions. Perhaps more
importantly, he was also a combination taxi driver, social
secretary, and confidante of the fashion icon Diana Vreeland,
who served the Met's Costume Institute as a consultant from
1972 until her death in 1989.

Mrs. Vreeland adored Richard and trusted his instincts, so I
was accepted as an intern. This four-year apprenticeship slowly
but completely transformed my life. This was where my real
education in design and the world of fashion took place.

With a collection of over thirty-five thousand costumes and
accessories spanning five continents and as many centuries, The
Costume Institute is among the most preeminent institutions of
its kind worldwide. It is home to five thousand square feet of
galleries, one of the world's foremost fashion libraries, design
archives, fashion prints, drawings, photographs, sketchbooks,
and more. It captivated me instantly. It was a combination fashion
laboratory-graveyard-purgatory-heaven all rolled into one.

Up until this point in my life, the only noncontemporary
clothes I had ever seen were at the Salvation Army, thrift
stores, and flea markets. I had never been exposed to fashion
at this grand level. At The Costume Institute, I literally had

a history of fashion laid out before me in a glorious time line. Best of all, this was history that I could feel as well as see.

The start of my internship unfolded slowly, like layers. As I got to know my way around that labyrinth of fashions, the people in charge of the Costume Institute began to see what I was good at doing. Some of my first duties included researching information on a particular garment being prepared for an exhibition. I would try to uncover and report on the history of the outfit, who had worn it, and so forth, so that information could be incorporated into the exhibition. Any and all of this background detail is essential, because it helps to inform the way a dress will be displayed, and tells the bigger story of society and of history itself.

On my way to and from the Costume Institute, which is situated in the basement of the giant structure that is the Met, I loved walking past the remnants of time from all over the world and every period in human history. Interning at the museum brought me closest to the thing I loved most, which was art. I especially appreciated walking out late at night, when the museum was closed to visitors, and passing the mummies.

With the dim lighting and the solitude of the empty corridors, how lucky I felt to have a private audience with these kings and queens. I loved how the linen had been wrapped around the mummified remains and had barely disintegrated over centuries. There was an aching, timeless beauty in the way those fabrics were wrapped and overlaid, and in how the various white, cream, yellow, and brown stained fabric strips marked the passage of time.

How magnificent and dignified those remains are, I thought, and how one with the cloth that wrapped and protected them. Just walking past the mummies, sphinxes, and all of their jewelry and accoutrements wove me into the quilt of the magnificent through the magic of time.

MY INTERNSHIP AT THE MET corresponded to the final years of the great Diana Vreeland's tenure at the Costume Institute. Her fashion exhibitions had become world-famous events, part social happenings, art openings, and cultural phenomena. They became premier New York events, where Downtown met Uptown and art met fashion.

This suited Mrs. Vreeland well, since this mood and point of view were what she had achieved at *Vogue* magazine, where she served as editor-in-chief during most of the 1960s and early 1970s. With Mrs. Vreeland at the helm, *Vogue*'s pages were designed to transport readers, presenting a smorgasbord of culture that offered art, world news, fashion, beauty, politics, witty nonsense, and thought-provoking views on life in general. The magazine was extremely influential and reflective of the vibrancy of American life at the time.

Before coming to *Vogue*, Mrs. Vreeland had served as a fashion editor at *Harper's Bazaar*. Starting in the 1930s, she helped define the eccentric, surreal, experimental, and exotic tone of fashion's high life over the next three decades. With inspired wit and knowledge, her point of view became a cultural landmark and point of reference in fashion that lingers to this day. Her fearless and determined eye, and her genuine enjoyment of fashion and life, still provoke applause and wonder from young fashion enthusiasts all over the world. She let fashion be fun, yet took it very seriously, knowing that fashion, like art, has a profound impact on the human mind.

Knowing that fashion is everywhere and carries with it so much responsibility, it's no wonder that Mrs. Vreeland's influence caused her to plunge into politics, and specifically into the White House. At the start of the 1960s, as Jacqueline Kennedy was about to assume the role of First Lady of the United States, it was Diana Vreeland's eye and advice that guided Mrs. Kennedy and helped the world fall in love with Jackie's mind and spirit.

The work at the Met was exhausting and demanding. Some nights after work, we would all pile into a limousine and drive out to Coney Island with Richard and Mrs. Vreeland to eat the most delicious pizza. This well-kept secret that Richard knew about on Neptune Avenue was well worth the trek. They grew their own tomatoes in their backyard. It was one of many cheap but glamorous dates to originate at the Met.

THE COSTUME INSTITUTE'S EXHIBITION GALLERIES seemed to go on for miles, winding this way and that way. By the end of my internship there, Mrs. Vreeland was being wheeled around the galleries in a wheelchair so that she wouldn't have to walk so far when inspecting the shows being mounted. Even from her wheelchair, though, Mrs. Vreeland's posture, carriage, and gestures were all beautifully choreographed to project style

at its best. She was usually decked out in a severe black
turtleneck and smart black pants. When she bolted
out of the wheelchair, her stride and
body language commanded attention.
Often, I focused on her tiny, elegant feet,
which were often encased in the most exotic shoes in any
glorious color other than sensible black.

Mrs. Vreeland's office in the basement of the Met
had no windows and was painted bloodred.
Like Mrs. Vreeland herself, this intimate
room was full of marvelous information.
The walls and desktop were layered
with notes, sketches, and photographs.
Anywhere your eye landed, it was clear
that this woman was an enormous
force in the fashion world. She was
much more knowledgeable about
clothes than anyone else I'd ever met, and
she had endless stories to share with the curators
and volunteers about the designers and ateliers who
had crafted the clothes we worked on. She also spoke
about the lifestyles lived by the people who had worn
these garments through time, serving as a walking
textbook of fashion history for the rest of us.

What I loved
about Mrs. Vreeland
was her enthusiasm
and curiosity for fashion. She viewed
fashion not from just a business
perspective, or even a historical
one, but from the personal point
of view of a woman of fashion.
She really wanted to know how
certain clothing was made and
how it felt to wear it. She knew
that the act of wearing is where
fashion comes to life, because that is
the ultimate collaboration between
the couturier and the client.

For instance, she was fascinated by my footwear. Mrs. Vreeland was mad about shoes, the more exotic the better, and we shared the same shoe size. She once noticed a pair of high-heeled galoshes I was wearing, and after that moment, she always looked at me from the feet up to get the news.

Another time, I was wearing two pairs of shoes at once—a pair of kid leather gold sandals inside a pair of Ruben's large, rubber tire–soled sandals—and Mrs. Vreeland could *not* resist asking me to take off my shoes and let her try them on.

"I want to see what it's like to walk with two pairs of shoes," she explained.

I slipped out of my shoes, handed them over to her, and she walked around the galleries in my sandals inside Ruben's, exclaiming at the novelty of the sensation. She adored the clumping sound of the two pairs of sandals colliding with each other. "Like a downtown Japanese Geisha!" she marveled.

Mrs. Vreeland's genuine interest in couture, and her enthusiastic appreciation of the craftsmanship and hours of devotion that it took to create the clothing and accessories that form the costume collection at the Met, never diminished with time. In fact, her admiration for the art of fashion grew stronger as that lifestyle and that way of living faded into the past. It was evident to me that she was a cultural living treasure.

Mrs. Vreeland was also a living bridge to an era in history when much time and energy was devoted to personal appearance and presentation. This required an army of passionate, committed professionals and talented artisans from a broad spectrum of diverse industries who were all at the service of the fashionable women who could afford to indulge in this passionate art form. These women were collecting the art of fashion. Luckily for us, museums have preserved these works of ingenuity and artistry.

This firsthand history lesson made me realize that fashion allows you to cross into another time in history, and into other cultures and societies. By examining fashions of a certain period, one learns about what was happening socially, politically, and economically.

Upon closer inspection, fashion's weave expresses the intimate proximity that cloth has with civilization. In history, you can literally trace the growth and progress of a society through its garments. Much the same way, you can follow the physical development of a person's size by the taking in and letting out of the seams in that person's clothing. In a throwaway society, we can see society's habits in the value it places on the importance of the quality of consumption. Clothing really reflects who we are and what we aspire to be.

These lessons in fashion history were made only more relevant for me because Mrs. Vreeland had worn so many of these clothes herself, or had known most of the women who did, as well as the designers who had made them. This personal intimacy with fashion, along with her firsthand accounts of where these clothes had been worn, what kinds of lives these women led, and why they needed these particular kinds of clothes and this level of luxury, is what made fashion history come to life for me. When you understand that clothing answers a particular need for women and when fashion fulfills and supplies the unexpected solution of what to wear, this is what justifies fashion in the end. The fact that women need and desire these clothes in their lives is the ultimate validation of fashion design.

• • •

I RELATED TO THE SAME passion Mrs. Vreeland spoke of, and
felt that I had the vision to partake in this art form and add a
different voice to the discussion. The richness of the culture
of fashion depends on the variety and diversity of ingredients
that go into it. I was beginning to discover how patterns
repeat themselves in fashion and history, and how I could add
something new to this world.

For example, to discover that Empire style dresses, with their high waists, first appeared in the late 1790s was at first a pleasant surprise because it was exactly that style that all the hippie teenage girls were wearing when my sisters and I arrived from Cuba. I also learned how influential the French government had been in developing the art of couture and building up a fashion empire. In the early 1800s, when Napoleon was determined to have France become the world's fashion leader, he forbade the women in his court to appear in the same dress more than twice. This was a clever way to increase consumer spending; it was hard on the pocketbook but a pleasure for the eyes. After Napoleon returned from Egypt, the fashionable ladies added embroidered borders to their hems, mimicking the silhouettes seen on hieroglyphic panels.

Fashion history owes a lot to Napoleon's wife, Empress Josephine, who knew the power of fashion and how to use it to advance a cause or to fashionably spread a political idea. It was curious to see how many times fashion was woven into history, and how cloth entered political policy, as when Napoleon halted the import of British textiles and revived French lace making.

The examples of French lace especially appealed to me. French lace is vulnerable and intimate, unlike the protective and dense character of Swiss lace, which can be heavy like armor.

I have always loved lace. Perhaps my affinity for lace is genetic, since on my mother's side my aunts were expert embroiderers and lace makers. It was traditional for a young woman in Cuba to have her lace garments and embroidered linen made for her wedding trousseau. Now, in examining lace garments at the Met, I developed an even deeper respect for lace than before, never suspecting that I would someday become not just a part of fashion history, but a part of world history, when I used an exquisite Swiss lace for First Lady Michelle Obama's dress and coat over thirty years later!

Lace appeals to me because it is fragile and strong at the same time; it is at once ancient and modern. I sought lace whenever I went fabric shopping. Once, I found a supply of vintage cotton lace in a sewing shop in West New York, and this is what I used to make my wedding dress years later. I'd also buy lace doilies in thrift shops and sew them together to make clothing, like lace patchwork dresses. I would learn to achieve lacelike effects by pulling the threads out of open-weave linens and gauzes. I still design lace items of every description, from jackets to coats, dresses to baseball shirts, and even shorts. I wear lace with just about anything, from carpenter's pants to T-shirts bibbed with it. That's why I consider it such a timeless, essential, and modern textile.

. . .

SINCE I KNEW WHAT WENT into the making of clothing, from the pattern making to the sewing and tailoring, I was overwhelmed by the collection at the Met. The level of expertise, dedication, and innovation was staggering.

Working so closely with these garments, I was able to witness firsthand the design language of each maker. The techniques the designers employed, the design lines, and their own particular ways of handling cloth are as evident to read as in the works of painters. A Matisse has its own linear rhythms, for instance, which are distinct from the lines of a Picasso or the colors of a Monet. The same is true of fashion designers who, consciously or not, infuse their work with their creative fingerprints.

Something inside of me clicked as I saw firsthand something that I had always sensed: Fashion design is—like painting or sculpture—an enduring art form with its own distinctive, exquisite language. Fashion can be elevated to the level of fine art.

When we fashion designers busy ourselves with our own visions, it's impossible not to leave our fingerprints and footprints embedded in the paths we're taking. You constantly retrace and revisit your design solutions for answers to new design questions as they arise. This creates grooves and tracks that are easily identifiable as their maker's. For me, that means that every time I create a new design, it is in hopes of discovering or sculpting a new letter that I can utilize and add to my personal design alphabet.

In all, Mrs. Vreeland organized a dozen of the Costume Institute's exhibitions between 1972 and 1984. She set a new worldwide standard with these and put fashion history and fashion museum exhibitions on the radar, helping to elevate the public's understanding of fashion as an art form. Her shows were legendary, truly giant spectacles that took up room after room, hall after hall in what seemed like the entire basement of the Met.

Mrs. Vreeland was creating a landscape for fashion history that one could traverse, traveling forward and then back again through time. The spectator could see and understand how all of the designs were connected, and how they related to the world at large. Artworks and furniture designs from the corresponding period were also in the Met's collection; they were shown side by side with the most inventive couture as part of the weave of each Costume Institute exhibit. In the four years that I was interning at the Met, I was privileged to work on *The Eighteenth-Century Woman*, *Royal Costumes of India*, and *Man and Horse*, among others.

Each of these exhibits required what seemed like a cast of thousands, or at least hundreds, of interns and volunteers to carry out and set up in time for the exhibition. At night, if Ruben arrived and came through the back door of the museum to pick me up, even he was put to work, helping to polish the silver of a maharajah's bed, or disassembling and cleaning the cubist glass beads from a giant Art Deco hanging chandelier, then putting them back carefully, one by one.

My sculpting skills were put to very good use. One of my duties was to sculpt and customize forms to fit the garments being exhibited. This was necessary because many of the historical pieces had distinct body shapes that would not fit any preexisting dress forms or mannequins. In addition, the couture dresses designed by Charles Frederick Worth, Paul Poiret, Christian Dior, Elsa Schiaparelli, Coco Chanel, and other greats had once belonged to particular women with specific body measurements.

Creating these mannequins and forms taught me about the intimate and trusted relationship that the couture houses have with their clients. The diversity of body types and proportions the designs had been engineered to fit was astounding. I could easily relate to this tradition, having grown up going with my mother to her seamstress, or *costurera*, to have our clothes made.

.   .   .

Although I was learning a lot as a research intern, I soon discovered a room called the "Conservation Laboratory." Better yet, *it* discovered *me*. In the mad rush to get these exhibitions ready in time, a good pair of extra sewing hands was always necessary and appreciated, much like the bridal shop episode back in my early teens.

The trusted seamstresses who restored the Costume Institute's valued garments were all ladies from the Upper East Side. They were my seniors, many the age of my grandmothers, who were surprised and pleased to discover that I knew all about fine hand-stitching and appreciated their talents. I especially loved darning by hand; one of the things that I admired most of all about the ladies at the Met was the way they backed and repaired a garment by darning it, almost mimicking the cloth—something most museums don't do any longer. The science and technology of restoration has eliminated this process.

Being at the Met and seeing all of these masterful textiles and constructions, I still hadn't been able to fully grasp this world of cloth, women, function, society, and glamour and see how it might relate to my potential future. Once I was gifted with the rare opportunity to restore the insides of some of the garments being prepared for exhibitions, however, I was literally holding that privilege between my hands. This was like opening up Pandora's box.

In a way, this reminded me of how I had once loved taking apart my dolls, and now I had the chance to peek at the inner workings of these masterpieces of fashion I understood the secret language of many great designers, and having this firsthand dialogue with history gave me direction.

It was at the Met that I first encountered clothing by one of the designers to whom I'm most often compared, Madeleine Vionnet, who lived from 1876 to 1975. Vionnet was a true pioneer in the use of bias. Her deep understanding of the true nature of different fabrics allowed her to recognize that cloth falls differently depending on whether you cut it across, with, or against the grain. Her technical breakthroughs in the art of dressmaking, which for me border on the scientific, were major stepping-stones and part of the ongoing design dialogue of fashion.

At the height of her career, Vionnet employed over a thousand workers and took good care of all of them, providing not only great working conditions, but health benefits as well. This fact has always been a real inspiration to me. When your work and your aesthetic can be so well aligned to how you manage your business, every square inch of effort can be enjoyed by all and will be rewarded in the long run.

I also came to appreciate the work of Madame Grès, also known as Alix, who first made her name in the 1930s by creating finely pleated, sculptural dresses. She designed dresses well into the 1980s and, like Vionnet, pushed the boundaries of fashion and taste with her concepts and technical skills. This is where real fashion innovation happens, and where the art of fashion is pushed forward.

I was also privileged to see the interior workings of a Dior corset and feel the soft sculpture of a Balenciaga coat—all masterpieces of engineering and craft that are not always evident from the outside, but created for the wearer's ease and comfort as well the splendor of the total effect. The language I came across in these interiors had a resemblance to the blueprints of an engineer's plans.

My internship was the most rewarding fashion education that I could ever have wished for, because it was a complete circle of knowledge. Fashion is an intangible, ephemeral discipline. That's what makes it such a fascinating art, but at the same time, an art that is difficult to fully grasp and understand.

Since I spent months preparing the clothes to be shown on mannequins and forms, and building up the forms to support the dresses, I was able to experience the work of all of the fashion greats firsthand and from the inside out. I came to know and understand their own particular skeletons. Each designer had their own very individual signature, their own way of forming their ideas into a dress. I began to clearly understand why their names and stories became fashion legends, and why their work is still so relevant today.

Each creator arrived at their own signature by embedding their intention in the work itself. That intent is what gives the work its form. Designers shape their ideas through their understanding and appreciation of craftsmanship, and through their ability to demonstrate a particular expertise. I learned at the Met that a dress is much more than what you see on the surface.

Nothing else that I may have done or studied at that time could have taught me more about the art of fashion than my time at the Met, not only because the legendary Mrs. Vreeland was at the helm, with her pertinent, firsthand knowledge, but also because this experience allowed me to begin viewing fashion as part of culture in general. At the Costume Institute, fashion was treated as one of the arts worthy of study, and regarded as one of the pieces of the puzzle that distinguishes a society at any given point in time. My experiences there helped me view fashion design in context among the other artistic accomplishments of certain time periods, such as painting, sculpture, furniture design, and photography.

Today, I advise young fashion designers that
the best investment they can make in their
futures is to take the time to study what other
makers have done through the ages. You cannot
learn to have a creative vision. This flows from
inside you. With enough curiosity, practice,
and experimentation, your creative voice will
come through you naturally, woven out of the
threads of your own life experiences. However,
you will be more adept at translating your vision
into a thing of quality if you expose yourself to
the deep and fascinating collection of textiles,
workmanship, and craft that is fashion history.
By understanding the process of making, you
will eventually arrive at your own design DNA.

After years of investigative curiosity and necessary problem solving, we designers leave behind a trail of clues to our thought process. This is our personal design language. Fashion's weave, when studied closely, reveals all of life and society in its tucks and seams and accumulates the hopes and ideals of our times. This is why I say that fashion is what time looks like.

It has been my great privilege to contribute to the living time line of history that is fashion, all linked together stitch by stitch to form our human story. By nurturing my love of art, I encountered my strength and focus. For me, the act of creating is the most essential part of life's journey, compelling me forward garment by garment. In the end, it is never futile to feed your passions. What you're really doing is replenishing your soul.

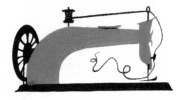

6 Marrying Love and Art

Staying raw means leaving room in

your life for the new.

I HAVE ALWAYS LOVED THE RAW

in me. I'm comfortable with the unknown

and with its mystery. In my work, I'm

constantly trying to discover a way to

solve new design challenges. That's what

inspires me to keep making things that

surprise me.

Staying raw means leaving room in your life for the unexpected and unperfected. The raw in you is often the most sincere response. There will be enough time later to refine and edit, but to keep the raw flowing, all of your life is a treasure. When your life partner appreciates the raw in you, too, that's divine.

ART AND LOVE

During the time that I worked at the Met, Ruben and I fell ever more deeply in love. Our lives became increasingly intertwined. We had a euphoric ardor for art and for each other that was wonderfully nourishing, especially because we shared every aspect of our life and love. Art reflects life, and life reflects art, so this was love at its fullest.

This very nurturing time was the essence of what it means to grow into yourself and into each other, separate but very together, and to intertwine like two healthy vines. We did not think of art as a career or a profession; it was simply a way to live and breathe. We were both captains of our own ships—or at least of our rubber rafts, as we floated, or sometimes ran the rapids, in this new wave of culture swirling all around us like a giant whirlpool of new impressions and ideas, sights and sounds.

We are all born with that secret key that gives you the power to unlock your ideas. Ruben and I were extremely lucky in that we not only found our secret keys to creativity as children, but also found each other along the way and could fully share our curiosity and wonder. The fact that we were both transplanted immigrants really provided us with a clean slate, from which we could organically grow into our new shapes without any preconceived ideas or road map.

While I was furiously absorbing everything I could at the Met, Ruben had found his way into working retail jobs that provided him with steady cash, yet gave him enough freedom in his schedule to flex his creative muscles on other projects. I got quick peeks into this funky retail environment whenever I picked him up from work at the end of the day.

Ruben first worked at Unique Clothing Warehouse downtown on Broadway, which was a superinnovative fashion warehouse full of army surplus finds. His job was to go down into the subbasement, which was below the subway, and dig through giant wooden crates full of uniforms from World

War II, Hawaiian shirts, WAC suits, flight suits, and every other sort of wonderfully made and excellently designed work clothes that had been forgotten by time.

The items Ruben dug up were sold in Unique's cramped, wooden-floored shop that reeked of fashion possibilities. Unique was such a hot spot for trend spotting and low-cost treasures that it was constantly filled with faces who were making news all over the world.

Ruben learned to be a salesman at Unique as well, which really helped him grow out of his shyness and prepare him for things to come. He assisted Grace Jones, who came in shopping with Issey Miyake, the great designer from Japan. Ruben helped find orange nylon jumpsuits for all of the band members of Devo when they were in town from Ohio to play a concert, and he met Fred Schneider of the super-stylish B-52s, who had just released their big hit, "Rock Lobster," and were hunting down looks for their next tour.

Ruben was especially starstruck, as were his coworkers at Unique, when the singer Diana Ross came in for a summer vacation wardrobe. The shop stayed open late to let the legendary star and her kids shop without getting mobbed by fans. As a thank-you for clearing out the store and staying open late just for her, Ms. Ross even sang an impromptu concert for the staff while trying on and modeling her army surplus shorts, regulation sailor top, and Cold War trench coat!

RUBEN AND I WERE BLESSED to come of age in the open, creative atmosphere of New York City in the late 1970s. Although not a genteel place, especially not downtown Manhattan, New York City always felt like a very human village because it was such a gritty, raw place. At that time, Union Square Park was boarded up and fenced in like a war zone. Bryant Park, behind the New York City Public Library, was a no-man's-land too dangerous to walk through even during the daylight hours—a far cry from what it has become today, a park overflowing with flowers and outdoor cafés that served as the posh home of Fashion Week until recently, when Lincoln Center replaced it as Fashion Week's venue.

Because of this raw feeling in New York City, the energy level and opportunities for young artists seemed truly endless. Not to mention the cheap rents one could find. For us, the City has always represented the mythical Land of Oz, radiating and attracting its own creative energy, as if there were a permanent sign over it announcing, CALLING ALL ARTISTS!

New York's unique synergy between art, fashion, music, theater, performance, film, and culture has always made Ruben and me feel fortunate indeed. The people who surround us in our day-to-day lives really helped to form us. To this day, the experiences we had in the City during our early years as a couple inform our way of looking at life. For that, we will be forever grateful.

We grew up in a very inclusive moment in time, one where the vibrant society around us was truly a diverse, democratic quilt. You were not defined by your age, race, sexual preference, bank account, or education. What counted most was your individual creativity. Your personal spark of genius—however you might express it—*that* was your identity. This ingredient makes you realize how vast the scope of humanity is, and how endless the possibilities are. That is the gift of large cities, with their accidental and wonderful mix of people. The social mobility that this mixture of humanity promotes is key to a successful and innovative society that was most definitely alive and kicking during our formative years.

It was interesting to observe that, as the economy was getting worse at that time, creativity was bubbling over like a boiling pot of newness. There was a garbage strike and a transit strike at the same time, and to see what seemed like all of New York walking together past mountains and walls of garbage during rush hour was an event.

Ruben walked past both Jackie Kennedy Onassis and Yoko Ono during these walking marathons, and both women cracked a smile in his direction when he recognized them. This freedom from barriers, both creatively and socially, is an essential quality that Ruben and I try to live by, and nowhere was this climate more felt than in the Downtown Manhattan art scene we encountered.

This scene included everything from art openings in church basements, late-night social hall dance parties, and performances in places like the Mudd Club and Club 57. The atmosphere was one part cabaret and one part Little Rascals, with live entertainment always on the bill. At Club 57, one could see artist Keith Haring do a go-go dance while John Sex, with his mile-high white pompadour, crooned out a Frank Sinatra ballad.

This nightlife scene was like a three-ring circus. Designer Katy K belted out sexy siren country and western songs while wearing Elvis jackets she had made out of black velvet paintings sold on 14th Street. The ultra-talented Ann Magnuson and our friend Joey Arias would be doing a Dalí and Gala pastiche, and Klaus Nomi was evolving his futuristic operatic persona.

This free-flowing atmosphere is where and how new ideas have a chance to start and develop. This sort of diverse community of talents and cross-pollination of art forms comes to fruition and creates the next stage of culture in these uncontrolled, free-form environments. What was being dreamed up downtown then and there was what America would grow up to become thirty years later.

SINCE RUBEN WAS NOW COLLABORATING with Joey Arias and Klaus Nomi in their performances, there were endless opportunities for me to hone my creative problem-solving mind. For one performance of Joey's band, Mermaids on Heroin, for instance, Joey asked me to make him a costume. I designed a linen suit with disconnected sleeves and lapels.

Making the suit out of disconnected pieces allowed me more freedom to create a deconstructed tailoring. I was hearkening back to those paintings that I'd taken apart and interpreted piece by piece in high school. I made Joey's suit out of black linen and sewed the pieces on with gold thread, giving it a strong, beautiful, graphic impact. It was thrilling to see him onstage wearing something I'd made, and even more thrilling because the suit actually stayed together while he performed!

Both Joey Arias and Klaus Nomi, in particular, personified what it means to live out your art through performance.

Klaus Nomi was an exceptional and brave artist, true
and real, a dreamer but also a realist. His operatic voice,
combined with his futuristic take on the baroque, helped
define the whole spirit of the New Wave movement of the
late 1970s in New York, which was tragically cut short by the
AIDS epidemic in the soon-to-come 1980s. Klaus was to be
one of the early victims.

Klaus would ride the subways in full makeup, his face stark
white, with black lips, no eyebrows, and pointy tricornered
varnished hair, wearing old skinny blue jeans with a white
T-shirt and a black leather jacket. He was a curious rebel
without a cause or a space-age Elvis. His sense of humor was
superb and fearless.

Once, a drunken thug came up to Klaus on the Number 6
train and said, "Hey, man, are you from another planet?"

Klaus, without missing a beat, answered, "Beep beep!" in
a high squeaky voice and the thug stared and walked away in
disbelief.

With artists like Klaus and Joey, Ruben and I saw firsthand
how art knows no borders. The entire city was their canvas,
and life was the ultimate creation. We observed the lesson
that a creative idea can, and should be, allowed to develop and
engulf an entire space.

Whether I was helping them think about how their performances would achieve more impact through lighting, movement, or costumes, the same principles applied. The act of creation is always born from love: a love of doing and forming something that will transmit love. An artist must never be afraid to let love loose on the world, no matter what form that takes. For me, a lot of that love was easy to let flow into Ruben, the creative world he had introduced me to, and into my work. Every opportunity to collaborate, I welcomed.

This was all good training for things to come.

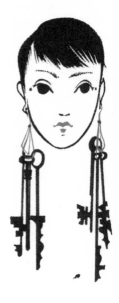

For another performance of Mermaids on Heroin at Danceteria, Ruben designed the stage set, entirely shrink-wrapping it in cheap red vinyl that he and I had bought on Canal Street, which at that time was an art supply paradise. I made costumes for the band out of shiny black vinyl and duct tape, as well as more than fifty black vinyl mermaid tails to represent oil-slicked mermaids. We proceeded to toss the mermaid tails from the high ledges around the club, even hanging them out of the windows of the building, swinging them over the lampposts outside and letting the tails spill off the awning over the club door.

As the dance scene began to slow down ever so slightly due to the death of disco, the start of the horrendous AIDS epidemic, and other factors, club owners started using their venues to host fashion shows, performance artists, movie screenings, and musicians to keep up the enthusiasm and deliver the unexpected to the nightlife audience. Now, instead of just going out dancing, Ruben and I were actually able to make some money

for doing what we loved. By day, Ruben was
now working at Parachute, an early fashion
retail pioneer in SoHo. By night, he helped
me organize kamikaze fashion shows in
unexpected places, like the bathrooms of
the Mudd Club and, later, at the Limelight.

I was still experimenting on myself all of
the time. Recycling and reappropriating materials
were necessary skills, due to finances, and very
useful when you needed to jump-start creativity.
To hold back my long hair, I hand-stitched red
plastic net onion bags into hair snoods that I paired with a severe
black turtleneck. I also made snoods out of
jockstraps I found on sale at Bargainland.

These reappropriated hair accessories
were documented by sharp-eyed Kim
Hastreiter of *Paper* magazine in one of
their earliest issues.

For jewelry, I strung fresh green and
yellow peppers together to form exotic,
delicious necklaces to spike up plain
white Hanes T-shirts. This was also
the first time that I started making
necklaces out of old keys of every shape

and metallic color possible. My mother had always saved lost keys, collecting them through the years, and I strung these together on cords and wires to assemble them into very heavy accumulations. These key collar necklaces eventually inspired a trend that continues in much more polished and lightweight versions to this day.

This world of creativity, collaborations, and newness was blossoming all around us. We were contributing to it, and it was feeding us both.

MARRYING ART AND LOVE

Suddenly, my free-flowing and trouble-free existence came to an end when my father died of an unexpected heart attack.

As everyone who has experienced the passing of a loved one knows, death can shake you to the core. Losing my father turned my world completely upside down. He had always been a steady figure in my life, one who helped me fine-tune my life compass. Whether we agreed on something or not, he always provided a point of reference.

I learned early on the importance of consistency from my parents. Whether they were right or wrong in my eyes, their consistency was what grounded me. I learned to navigate my

way around an issue, a conflict, or a point of view because
I could count on the base they provided. When all else
might shift in life, this sense of stability and consistency was
fortifying.

At the same time, I have always been logical and practical, and
when my father passed away, I became newly and keenly aware of
my life as an adult. I was the only child still living in my parents'
home, so I took it upon myself to assume the responsibilities of
my father's business, the building he had recently purchased, and
helping my mother through this transition.

Life now became a frantic series of decisions, all of
which I had to make according to unexplained, and often
incomprehensible, rules. Things were a lot less black-and-white;
there were now many hues of gray. The tempo of my life sped
up considerably. This sudden jolt of reality made it clear that I
was beginning a new chapter of adulthood, ready or not.

That same year, Ruben and I got married in a small
wedding full of love and hope, and the sun shone bright again.

PARTLY BY ACCIDENT, RUBEN AND I had not just one but three
weddings. But maybe this, too, reveals something about my
character, since in life, as in my work, I'm prone to ponder
and sit with an idea. Then, when I'm ready to articulate that

idea, I do so with unbridled commitment and enthusiasm!

Once we'd made the decision to wed, Ruben called City Hall to find out what we needed to do to get married. Then, armed with what a civil servant told him over the phone—"Come to Room 203," or something like that—we got dressed and took our parents along with us to be married in City Hall. For that wedding, I wore a tiny boy's pin-striped suit that I had altered to fit me, with a crocheted cotton lace veil and antique Victorian boots. On our way to the wedding, we were stuck behind a fourteen-wheeler truck that was holding up traffic. I knew that we had to make it to Room 203 before closing time at three o'clock, so I jumped out of the car, climbed up onto the window of the truck, and, in a slightly alarmed voice, said, "Move it! I'm late to my wedding!"

I must have been a sight in my veil, because it worked. The trucker stepped on the gas, and the traffic soon flowed!

Alas, it wasn't until we arrived at City Hall that we discovered that Room 203 was only the place where you fill out the application for an official wedding license, not a place where we could get married! The very kind lady in the window broke the news to Ruben in a hushed tone. Ruben convinced her to go with the flow and, rather than spoil this magical moment for our families, we completed the necessary paperwork, stepped away from the window, and announced to our families that we were now husband and wife.

After many tears of happiness, much rice throwing, and a few pictures, Ruben and I drove off for our honeymoon in Canada armed with a tank of gas and a road map. We were living in sin, but deliriously happy. The car we had inherited from my father had an ignition problem; when it was turned off, it was hard to start it again. This meant that the less we stopped the car, the better, so we drove and drove as many hours as possible, covering much lovely and fertile Canadian ground.

Our first stop was the magnificent Niagara Falls, where we stayed in the quietest, most time-forgotten bungalows. We were lucky to bump into them, as they were situated off the side of a high road with a startlingly charming and impressive view. The view wasn't of the Falls—that would have been way out of our budget. Instead, our view was of the tumultuous, whirlpool-filled waters at the base of the Falls. This was in April, not the high season for Niagara Falls, so we had the whole place to ourselves. It was the most romantic, intimate honeymoon I ever could have imagined.

We drove off from there to explore Canada, a country we adore for its sense of space and pace. Because it was early spring, it was still snowing; once we managed to get the car heater turned on high to thaw ourselves out, it got stuck there and we couldn't turn it off. The car got so hot inside that we resorted to stripping down to our underwear while we drove into the wild.

At one point, we got caught in a storm on a major mountain highway. The windshield wipers of our old car conked out with the weight of the blowing snow. Ruben drove at sixty miles per hour with his head poking out of the open window so that he could see until we found the next exit and could pull off the highway and wait out the storm.

We drove on and on, looking at the map only to decide what major geographic point we would head for next, and happily getting lost along the way. The views and lakes and mountains are still unforgettable memories, not only for their visual beauty and totally charming atmosphere, but because also for the new husband-and-wife life we were leading.

We weren't sure about where we were going, but we were absolutely thrilled to be going there together.

Soon after our return to New Jersey, and now armed with the proper papers, Ruben and I were secretly married in a civil ceremony with my middle sister, Mary, and Ruben's brother, Roberto, as our legal witnesses. They had to keep it secret so that our parents wouldn't realize that we'd gone off on our honeymoon without ever being married.

A month later, we had a proper church wedding, and that is the date that our families remind us of every year so that we can celebrate. We can't be blamed for forgetting our wedding anniversary after all of that.

Our church wedding was a very low-key affair. It was a warm summer day and we were surrounded by friends and family. Because of the recent loss of my father, emotions were running high and there wasn't a dry eye left in the church or outside. It was raining cats and dogs that afternoon—a sign of a long and happy marriage, lucky for us!

Ruben wore a steel gray suit that he had found at Salvation Army. The suit fit him perfectly. It had been tailored in Hong Kong, with the name of its original owner written on the label and discreetly sewn into the interior of the front pocket. As is the custom with tailored suits, the date it was completed was also noted: April 1961. This was the month and year that Ruben was born, so he took this as his good luck charm. He handpicked my bouquet of purple lilacs in a park that morning on his way to the church.

For my part, I captured my intense emotional state in that wedding dress. I made it from a humble crocheted cotton lace, a very fragile but sturdy web of stringlike lace that was light enough to catch a summer breeze. I draped the lace over a gauzy blue underslip in an overall apron design, with built-in lace belt loops and large patch pockets. That dress was symbolic of how lovely, blue, optimistic and hopeful I felt.

STARTING A LIFE TOGETHER

Ruben and I have opposite aesthetics and personalities in many ways, but we are intrigued and many times amused by each other's work habits and points of view. He works in total chaos, with a loud sound track to his day, which is totally opposite from my desire for peace and monklike tranquillity. I am not quite sure how it works but the atmosphere compromises and shifts according to the strongest natural vibe in the room. There are moments in my tranquil state when the sound of Ruben's tempo fills me with energy and possibilities. I give Ruben the peace he needs sometimes to focus.

How do we support each other's work? We don't. Our individual expression is just that: our own. Some of the dresses I make spook Ruben out, but these ugly ducklings patiently survive the guillotine. Those complex ideas often become the source later for building whole new collections.

I soon discovered that Ruben and I start from very different places when we make something. Now that we were living together, I had many opportunities to watch Ruben at work. I learned a great deal by doing so. Ruben creates in what seems like an impulsive way to many. He is fearless in his approach and works on total instinct.

To me, though, there is a wonderful grace, humor, and fluidity in the way Ruben throws himself onto a canvas. I found watching him work to be immensely satisfying and inspiring. He quickly taught me not to be afraid of empty space when you start making something, because of how he owns his artistic space immediately.

Watching Ruben draw—something I've always loved to do, since that freshman year art class at our high school—inspired me to create entirely new patterns, because of the fluid way his unconscious gestures helped me see movement and think about new ways to capture motion in fabric. Ruben's state of working bliss is an unconscious one. How can you tamper with that? You don't.

When I design, I create internally and meticulously. I think this stems from my practical nature. My mind constantly thinks of the most logical way to achieve. I make sense of space and how I am going to dress it. Rather than jump into doing a design, I think about it for a long time, until I know that I can create efficiently. My patterns reflect this: They have to be smart and fit the cloth. I cut practical, streamlined patterns after first thinking about how I'm going to approach them and envisioning the design in my head.

I approach fabric in the same way a sculptor studies a piece of stone before starting to chip away at it, very slowly and gently transforming raw material into art. I contemplate fabric visually and in a tactile way, understanding its language and alchemy before slowly directing the fabric and molding it into a garment. For me, a masterful, exciting design results when you watch the fabric do ninety-nine percent of the work.

In addition, I had begun to learn that another fundamental aspect of my designs was a deep appreciation of gravity and space. Working at the Met with garments crafted by so many different brilliant designers, along with making my own clothes, gradually taught me that gravity has the ability to transform a garment because of its effect on the fabric. As a designer, I was becoming increasingly aware of this invisible force, knowing that a dress in a certain fabric could look completely different from how I had envisioned it would look, once gravity entered into the equation and affected both the wearer and the cloth.

CREATING UNION AND TESTING OUR RETAIL IDEAS

During this period of time after our wedding and my father's death, we lived with my mother in West New York and kept my father's store going in Union City. We decided that it was time to make a change in the store because the wholesale business was drying up. We began by renaming it Union.

My father had been thinking about what he could do next with the shop because of the change he could see coming in retail. We decided to seek new resources and try to find a new clientele. Ruben was able to buy some leftover stock from his old boss at Parachute. We carried Kenneth Cole shoes because of another contact we'd made. To complement the stock we brought in from Parachute and other wholesale sources, I started making my own designs to sell.

At this particular time, I was focused on making layered gauzy dresses, because I was trying to find a way to make experimental clothes that were affordable for our customers, but could still generate at least a small profit for us. These simple gauzy dresses could be bought one at a time, and looked great when layered color over color. You could buy one and save up to buy another a week or two later, until you owned the whole collection. Each client could customize her look according to her particular style, which is just what people did. There was a high school in the neighborhood, and this idea was very compatible with the budget of our new young clientele. These dresses contained the seeds of a lot of my design ideas that I continue to evolve to this day.

I was still sewing clothes on the same old green Singer sewing machine that my father had given me so many years before. That machine was a workhorse and I loved it, since it was strong enough to sew even through denim. Ruben would sell the clothes upstairs, and he'd help me cut the cloth and iron the clothes at night after the store closed.

ONCE MY MIDDLE SISTER HAD her first baby, she was ready to take over the shop and manage the building. Ruben and I knew it was time for a move into Manhattan. We still didn't have much money, so the place we found was in Hell's Kitchen. This brought us physically closer to being completely broke. After we married, Ruben had stopped working his retail jobs to help out in the Union City store, but now he needed to generate a steady paycheck to pay the rent. He tried to "join the human race," as Ruben puts it, but found it difficult at first.

He found a job at Jezebel's, a soul food restaurant in the theater district. A lively place, this restaurant employed only the most innovative and theatrical-looking waitresses; with Ruben being the only busboy, the pay was generous enough to pay the rent and help us invest in our work.

In the amazing way that New York City has of weaving together lucky breaks, Ruben met a Frenchwoman named Maripol while she was having dinner at Jezebel's. Maripol was a talented artist, film producer, stylist, and photographer who had just opened a shop on Lafayette Street where she sold the jewelry she designed. She was probably best known as Madonna's stylist—Maripol was the one who created the trademark black rubber bracelets and crucifix jewelry for Madonna's *Like a Virgin* tour.

One of Maripol's responsibilities was to find young designers to showcase at Fiorucci. This designer concession stand was set up to expose New York to new talent right on the selling floor. Ruben showed some of my designs to Maripol, and she had the nerve to offer us that opportunity on the spot.

We took her up on the offer, since Fiorucci had been such good luck for Ruben before.

It was a great opportunity, although we were not making any money up front. It was a large investment to produce enough clothes for a month of selling, which was how long you were given at the concession stand. The pressure was on, since Maripol had gone on pure instinct to book me, the people at Fiorucci were giving us a prime spot in the center of the lower level of the store, and our friend Joey Arias was the main attraction at the front door of the store. We would have to do a lot to rise to this occasion.

And rise we did. We made fixtures out of giant pieces of driftwood we had collected from the Jersey shore and painted them in glossy neon yellow and neon orange. And, in record time, I managed to make enough dresses, handbags, accessories, and other curious fashion doodads to fill up our spot. The clothes were mostly sheer dresses and coats that I made out of colorful burlap lined in contrasting dark blue voile. I also created one of my favorite designs of the year: a burlap beach ball bag made out of three different colors.

My creations looked surreal, suspended and floating from the driftwood. It was exciting to see all of my ideas hanging together, and to watch the different types of people who chose to try on my clothes. This education in retail reality is a

valuable lesson for any designer. Fashion is one part fantasy, one part concept, and then there is the reality of fit, proportion, and construction. When all those elements happily collide with reality, you get to make a sale!

Our concession stand at Fiorucci was surrounded by stands featuring other designers, like Katy K, who made outrageous country western clothes and the best raincoats cut from 1950s shower curtains with printed poodles and mermaids. Laura Wells, who later opened the famous vintage shop Screaming Mimi's, also ran a concession stand there. She sold the most remarkable vintage shoes and bags, and her salesgirl went on to become one of the most talented voices of the time: Cyndi Lauper.

Ruben and I ran the concession stand as often as we had time for, and eventually made enough money to hire a shop assistant to sell the clothes when we couldn't be there. Joey came to the rescue when that time came, by finding us an adorable farm girl from Wisconsin named Suzie Zabrowska, a model, artist, filmmaker, and performer who often modeled in the windows of Fiorucci's and other stores.

Suzie was a great saleswoman, selling out most of our stock in no time. We became lifelong friends, and she went on to model in most of my early shows. Since she was a filmmaker, Suzie not only modeled in the shows, but filmed them while doing so. You can see some of this early footage on YouTube today, as a precious record of the early 1980s downtown fashion scene in New York.

WHILE THE FIORUCCI EXPERIMENT WAS in full swing by day, I still tried to help out at the Costume Institute whenever I

had the time. I loved the professional environment and my colleagues there, like Simon Doonan, who had come from California to work on the exhibitions; he was just about to start working at Barneys New York as their creative director. Simon's eye and wit were already in full bloom. He was about to unleash his stylishly outrageous point of view onto New York City streets via the windows of Barneys.

Besides running the Fiorucci concession stand, Ruben was also working at temporary art jobs. There were plenty of interesting, but not steady, opportunities for artists. The dance club Area was in full swing, and Ruben found his way there. Area was a dance club like no other, changing themes and scenarios monthly. The openings were packed with nightlife and art lovers. The club itself was an art installation. As with Mrs. Vreeland's costume exhibitions at the Met, it took a cast of many artists and creative construction workers to accomplish Area's monthly makeovers in time for the openings.

After the monthlong experiment at Fiorucci, we decided that we were ready to tackle something bigger. Ruben had always had faith in my vision and my work as a designer. At Fiorucci, we had experienced enough success selling my designs to know that my ideas worked at the retail level, and not just as art. Armed with this faith and knowledge, in 1984

Ruben took some of the dresses that I'd made for myself out of my closet and started to lay down the road toward our next frontier by showing them around at some of the most innovative stores in the city.

During this time, we were caught up in the washing machine of life, being spun round and round by our circumstances. We had no specific mold to break out of, but no time to be idle, either. We were busy generating our own existence with no time for reflection. We had only the raw ideas. There was no time for perfecting things yet, or even polishing up our thoughts. All of that was yet to come.

All ideas have to start somewhere, and that somewhere is sometimes a very raw place. Your imagination needs to be free of editing. The urge to create should never be burdened with perfection. This is the importance of appreciating every stage of your life and work. You will never be in the exact same place again. These raw seeds you will nurture to fruition soon enough.

Part **3** fashion ...

7 Breaking In

Learn to generate your own existence.

FOLLOWING YOUR INSTINCT IS

not difficult—it's shutting out all of the

other noise that's key. You have to find

the environment that allows you to focus

and feel clear enough to hear your own

thoughts. If you can't find it, you have

to form these surroundings yourself. You must generate your own existence.

ESTABLISHING THE HOUSE OF THE SELF-TAUGHT

I was coming from my own design vision. My experience up until 1985 had been to dress emotion. My take on a design line came from the need to graphically describe a feeling.

For instance, my obsession early on with cutting wavelike hemlines gave me the sensation of speed. Likewise, I would try to visualize what hugging arms looked like in cloth. My instinct when designing something was to focus on my strength: creating clean, bold shapes that enveloped the human body in new and surprising ways. I wanted to capture the abstraction and free-form emotion of jazz in cloth.

I had absorbed very useful information at both Parsons and FIT, where I exposed myself to the industry standards of the Seventh Avenue fashion world. I felt a bit overwhelmed by the prospect of working in the fashion industry, truthfully. It felt so large and fragmented that I couldn't see how I would fit into such large machinery.

Because I had been my own teacher for so long, the idea of turning my hobby and passion into a fashion business was too large to tackle all at once. By instinct, I sensed that I would have to learn the whole fashion cycle from the bottom up—or from the top down. No matter which way I did it, I knew that I would have to teach it to myself, step-by-step, in order to really grasp its form and successfully contribute another point of view.

Whether you decide to learn something from the bottom up, from inside out, or from whatever direction you choose to tackle it, the best way to teach yourself something new is to do it thoroughly, and not just as a casual observer. I want to make a point about the importance of being self-taught here. Believe me when I say that there is opportunity for those who don't fit in because they lack the inclination or tools to follow the industry's standard rules. There is still a place at the table for the outsider, and that's good, because outsiders enrich our culture.

FASHIONING A BUSINESS WITH SOUL

As most young married couples know, life is tough without a dowry. Living in love is a blessing in the same way that ignorance is bliss: You are high on that vibe of fulfillment until reality starts knocking on your door and asking for the rent.

Ruben likes to remind me that I married a poor starving artist who was rich in character and enthusiasm for his art, for his life, and for me, his new wife. Since Ruben had worked in and around fashion retail since he was sixteen years old, he had developed a great nose for newness and understood how much good fashion can inspire. He also had a sixth sense about my craft and was supremely confident about my talent. He knew, without a doubt, that my dresses had value that went far beyond dressing me.

Ruben walked out of our apartment one day with an armload of my dresses and a lot of faith in my work. His enthusiasm for my peculiar way of making clothes was his fuel. I trusted his instinct for my work, and he trusted mine as a maker.

The clothes that Ruben first showed to stores in
1984 truly reflected my own personal vision. They
were, in fact, my real wardrobe. Among them
was a navy blue jersey dress that was nothing
but a long tube with two giant patch pockets
and built-in loops to anchor to your
waist, all suspended from a roomy
funnel that mysteriously emerged
from the back to form a neckline. Every seam
on that dress was contrast-stitched like my
favorite blue jeans.

Ruben also took an aerodynamic,
red denim suit that was neat
and well behaved, except for the
exaggerated elbows cut with precision
into sleeve shapes. The lining of that
denim suit resembled a satin baseball
jacket made from the most delicious
colored silk. Each pattern piece was a
contrasting color. The surprise of the suit
was on the inside.

In a way, Ruben and I were lucky to have been
starting out in fashion completely self-taught and
learning it all from the ground up. The fashion

landscape of 1984 wasn't overcrowded with big brand names. Designers were not yet in the race for branding. Many designer names existed, but fashion wasn't yet such a huge corporate entity being traded on Wall Street.

The actual retail scene was much more diverse than it is today. The fact that so many privately owned boutiques existed also made fashion more interesting. A woman could visit different shops and find a diversity of design options, all relevant and different. Each boutique had its own buyers with their own tastes and points of view. You were bound to be intrigued and inspired to find something original that seemed tailor-made for you.

Even large shops, like Bloomingdale's, Bergdorf Goodman, Saks Fifth Avenue, and Henri Bendel were working hard back then to differentiate themselves from one another. This was how they developed a following. If they wanted their clients to return, they had to offer unique designs and things so new they weren't available anywhere else. Buyers were the explorers for the consumers, and new moods kept everyone interested.

This feeling of discovery is very good for business. Repetition tends to kill off the fashion urge after a while. The year that Ruben started showing my designs to stores, thankfully, the sense of seeking out the new was encouraged in the fashion retail world. New designers could make appointments and show their wares without having to leap a lot of hurdles. Fashion buyers had budgets they could spend according to their instincts, and this allowed them to take risks on new names and designs that looked promising.

WHAT DID THAT FASHION WORLD look like when we started out? By the mid-1980s, mainstream American fashion had become all about dressing the working girl. Meanwhile, MTV had burst on the scene, and was instantaneously bringing street fashions to the masses for the first time.

This was also the time of the power suit, which working women had embraced. Wall Street had met the Fashion District. This corporate uniform solidified and took on new cartoon proportions when the TV show *Dallas* hit the screen and shoulder pads invaded every inch of Seventh Avenue. From couture to Main Street, women were attracted to this silhouette, which had become the corporate fashion symbol. These pads were put into everything: sweatshirts, T-shirts, dresses, jackets, you name it. There were even do-it-yourself shoulder pad kits for your convenience.

When a fashion idea becomes as popular and overused as the power suit, design is usually ready to move on. I was proposing a more feminine, soft, and mysteriously dark silhouette. This was much less aggressive than what high fashion was championing at the time. Each generation dreams up the next decade, and I had started dreaming the nineties.

. . .

Ruben returned home from the streets that day with my clothes over his arm and two orders in his pocket. We were in business just like that! What was most striking was that the two shops placing orders with us could not have been more different in their clientele and fashion mission.

The first was Henri Bendel on Fifth Avenue. This had been a very high-end shop since the turn of the last century. Originally a milliner himself, Henri Bendel was the first buyer to bring Coco Chanel from Paris to the U.S., and the store had redefined the fashion retail scene in the 1960s by inventing what it called "The Street of Shops."

Instead of arranging itself like a traditional department store, Henri Bendel set up small, individual boutiques along its main avenue by the entrance. Shoppers could pop in and out of different fashion kiosks that lived side by side like spice shops. The merchandising idea wasn't about cohesion, but about options. At a time of individuality, a unified message would have killed the sale.

The clientele at Henri Bendel was very high-end—sophisticated, Old Guard New Yorkers who liked to wear elegant clothes with a slant toward the classics, and a bit of the exotic mixed in. The overall package was to classically dress the individual woman.

Ruben had heard that Henri Bendel saw designers once
a week in a sort of cattle call; they put each designer and his
or her clothes in a dressing room, and buyers would walk in
and out of the long row of fitting rooms to look at the clothes
hanging there. They had to be fast to cover as many designers
as they could in one morning, and had to trust their instincts.
In just the blink of an eye, they had to be able to spot a new
fashion possibility, a new business opportunity, and, hopefully,
the next "big thing." This would give them the edge on
other retailers. The chance to discover a look or a resource
that no one else had in New York was a mandate; business
opportunities therefore abounded for start-ups.

The second shop we took an order from that day was
Patricia Field on 8th Street. Her shop was already a legend
by the 1980s. She would change the look of the shop and the
merchandise according to her whim. It had been a futuristic
white cube, a rock-and-roll T-shirt store, and a New Wave
parlor. Keith Haring had painted directly on her windows,
which were at street level; you had to enter her shop by
descending a flight of stairs into a whole new world.

Patricia Field is a true genius retailer, with a brave eye
and a great instinct. She had come up with the idea of selling
Lycra pants for the roller disco world, for instance, way before
anyone knew they needed them. Later on, Pat would become

the style choreographer for the television shows *Sex and the City* and *Ugly Betty*.

Now, Pat was voting on my designs with her checkbook, placing an order that day on a new designer she had never heard of before. Retailers and fashion gurus like Pat Field, whose antennae are pitched so high, really move the fashion world forward. By marrying their business sense with fashion know-how, they provide a platform for fresh ideas and help create an exciting, ever-changing fashion landscape by exposing their clients to new designers. One of my first customers, I later learned from Pat, was the artist Francesco Clemente's wife, Alba Clemente. Alba wore dresses from Valentino, Yves Saint Laurent, and other couture masters. Now, through Patricia Field, she was introduced to my work as well.

Both of these shops placed orders for my jersey dresses and capes, and for my denim coats and suits. Those denim garments were the ones that would immediately cause a stir. They would be key to earning a wider notice for my designs in the fashion world.

Perhaps even more importantly, though, one of the key things that Ruben and I learned from this early retail experience was that the scope of interest in my designs encompassed different women who lived diverse lifestyles, from the art-loving, independent downtown clients at Patricia Field to the more classically dressed women of Henri Bendel's. The women who bought my clothes had sent me a personal message: I was free to flex my design muscles without the added burden of editing my creative gene. This message came at a very crucial time in my work and development as a young artist.

BIRTHING A BUSINESS FROM THE SCHOOL OF SELF-TAUGHT

I blame denim, in part, for my decision to enter the fashion business. I have always loved working in denim, not only because it was one of the most affordable fabrics at the time that I began working as a designer, but also because I love its tough industrial nature and integrity. It is an easy fabric to sew as long as you have the right tools. An industrial machine strong enough to tame this stubborn cloth helps.

But the most lasting attraction that denim has for me is its character. To me, the cloth represents the American spirit, and capturing that spirit is one of the original inspirations that caused me to want to step into the world of fashion. From the start, I felt the need to create garments that can last forever.

Even when something I make is new, it has to feel like it has a history.

I lined the denim suits and coats that I created for Henri Bendel and Patricia Field with silk satin patchwork fabrics in surprising kaleidoscopes of colors because, once again, I was drawn to the look of these luxury fabrics against the tough industrial denim, and I loved the pop of bright colors on the interior of a garment. I also loved the soft feel of the satin against the skin, because it was a complete surprise and a visual contradiction.

Looking back on those particular coats now, I can see how I was influenced to make them the way I did. Their design echoed the buildings I had known as a child in Camajuani, with their stark, stucco exteriors and the bright surprise of colored painted tiles decorating the inner rooms. I have always loved combining humble and luxury fabrics to create sensory surprises for the eye and skin.

Of course, I was used to making clothes only for myself; making that many dresses and coats to fill our orders from Patricia Field and Henri Bendel was going to be another matter altogether. With a firm order in hand, I needed to jump into action. I was thrilled to be in business, but a bit overwhelmed at the same time. It's one thing to make clothes for yourself, but quite another when you suddenly have orders for ten dresses due to be delivered in a week's time!

How was I going to do this? I had been sewing on my own for pure pleasure and self-expression. Sewing clothes for myself was a labor of love and an extension of who I was, but now I had to make patterns, grade different sizes, cut an entire order one by one, and deliver it on time—or risk a cancellation!

There were no hours to waste and no point in panicking. I needed to throw all of my limited life experiences and passion into a pot, stir them up, and get cooking. I am not one to shy away from a challenge, and this was a huge step that I was about to take.

Ruben and I have always embraced the importance of teaching ourselves what we need to know. Our experience has always been that if you don't teach yourself something you don't know, you might learn it wrong. Together, we now proceeded to teach ourselves how to produce an order of clothing destined not for my closet, but for women I had never even seen before.

We had no idea how to go about buying fabric wholesale, or how to buy zippers in bulk. These were the kinds of mundane but necessary details that help you understand how to price your garments. Even more difficult than that was the task of grading the patterns into different sizes to accommodate the orders.

We ran on pure adrenaline and Cuban coffee. I still had that same green Singer sewing machine my father had given me. Luckily, I also had Ruben and his parents. I taught Ruben how to do the pattern layouts and cut them out in the most efficient way on the fabric. I also taught him how to use an iron to do underpressing. Thankfully, the order was mostly denim, which was easy for him to handle.

We didn't own a cutting table, so we proceeded to map out and cut the entire order on the wooden floor of our apartment. Our two orders combined stretched from the living room, down the hall, and into the kitchen. We used cans of evaporated milk to weigh the fabric down and traced the patterns one by one with tailor's chalk. I chained myself to the sewing machine and stitched every piece. The production had to be done quickly to make our tight deadline, but the garments had to be as well made as I could possibly achieve.

Ruben couldn't resist drawing on the wrong side of the denim fabric since it would never be seen once it was lined. I love knowing today that, somewhere out there in the world, the insides of the early Isabel Toledo denim coats have hand-drawn profiles in tailor's chalk by Ruben Toledo.

We could not afford the minimum order needed for labels, and had no idea where we could have some made. Ruben's mom, Oneida, came to the rescue. She had worked at an embroidery factory in Union City and gave us a roll of ribbons embroidered with cats and bears that she had saved in the hopes of using them for future grandchildren. We proceeded to embroider the labels on the opposite sides with our own hand stitches, spelling out, "Isabel Toledo." These made for very naïve yet special labels, an unexpected nonindustrial finishing touch. Some of these early Toledo pieces occasionally turn up on eBay; examples from this early collection are easy to identify because of these handmade labels.

The first delivery to Patricia Field included car coats with curved hems hiking up the back of the knee. The pencil skirts also had curved hemlines that captured a continuous flow, making the eye travel from front to back in one sweep. These lines expressed my fascination with speed and movement.

Once again, I could recognize that I was tapping into the self-taught theory. My way of designing was linked to how I draped from the side of my own figure. Instead of looking at the human form from the front or the back, I was more in tune with its sides. Observing a garment from this angle, you are forced to take into account the rhythm of the line as it travels from front to back. I outlined these curvy, smooth lines in crisp double topstitching to clearly signify the intent of the lines.

Fashion journalists were a very hungry, curious lot in the mid-1980s. Like a fashion Sherlock Holmes, a fashion journalist was always on the lookout back then for new designers and collections that they might discover and report on first. So, when a reporter spotted my design in Patricia Field, Patricia gave my name to him. He happened to be a reporter from *Women's Wear Daily*, the bible of fashion trade journals, and he was intrigued enough by my clothes to want to find out who I was, and to write a story about my collection.

This was a really big event for me: To be written up in the industry's most important fashion business paper was a first. The reporter asked about the clothes, where they were produced, what the price range was, if I was planning to grow my business, and what I had in mind as a distribution strategy—all very industry-driven questions.

At the end of our interview, the reporter posed a follow-up question that I hadn't been at all prepared for: "Are you showing your next collection during Fashion Week?"

Until this point, Ruben and I had been traveling in completely different circles from most fashion designers. Although we were definitely involved in fashion culture, these were all fashion industry questions that we'd never considered before. We didn't have any idea what Fashion Week was!

However, when Ruben asked the reporter what Fashion Week might involve, we were informed that collections would be shown in a month's time. There was no time to rest on my new and hard-won laurels. It was back to the sewing machine for me.

THE FIRST SHOW GOES ON

Ruben and I worked feverishly for that first fashion show, determined to exhibit our own collection during Fashion Week. At one point, another reporter from *Women's Wear Daily* phoned to see if she could come by for a preview of the collection. I had nothing finished for her to view, so I had to tell her that I was just too busy to see her.

"Come back in three days," I said, figuring I'd have something completed and ready for her to see by then.

The idea of making a whole fashion collection in a single month was daunting and exhausting, but the creative challenge of presenting my vision of a new woman was pure joy. We again were lucky enough to be able to enlist our families' help in order to meet this new deadline.

When Ruben's dad, Vitelio, was a young man, his first job was at a shop in Old Havana called Kosack Tailors, which later changed its name to Atomic Tailors after the Revolution. When he entered the United States, he eventually found a job as a cutter in a New Jersey factory that made men's jockey shorts. He had learned to cut mountains of white cotton jersey into T-shirts and men's underpants with a giant industrial cutting blade. His experience and advice really came in handy now.

Vitelio bought me a double-needle sewing machine, which really saved me time. He also bought us some much-needed supplies. He introduced us to dotted paper, the kind you use for making patterns. He presented me with proper cast-iron weights, so that we could dispense with using our milk cans to hold the paper patterns on to the fabric. Vitelio also gave us a pair of electric cutting shears for using on tougher textiles, like denim and thick wools, when cutting more than one layer at a time—another great time-saver!

Since we couldn't afford to make printed invitations, we hand-embroidered the show information—the date, time, and location—on long white gloves we bought at a Goodwill store. We folded these elegant white gloves into envelopes and mailed them to a few people we had met in the fashion-business world. We were thrilled when *The New York Times* called those gloves "the season's best invitation."

For this first fashion show, we talked friends into lending us

their office on the corner of 57th Street and Fifth Avenue—a tiny space, but an ideal location. I understood the importance of location; this office would later be our first showroom.

That building now houses the prestigious, glamorous Louis Vuitton headquarters and store. But, in 1984, it was an Art Deco leftover dream, very elegant and austere. The long white marble hallways were outlined in black mosaic tiles, and led you into the tiny office where Ruben installed some quickly made ink drawings of naughty, sweet naked girls spelling out my name.

This was not to be a big production. We had to be able to come in, set up, and pack up in a matter of hours. Simple magic and practical reality reigned in all Toledo endeavors. There would be no rehearsals or planning. It all had to come through in one take, with no second chances possible. All we could be sure of was that this was a very lovingly well-made collection.

We did have a boom box that we had rehearsed perhaps a little too well. Ruben had played the tape of Cuban music we expected to use during the show so often that, while we were working on the collection, he wore the batteries down to the last drop of juice.

Our models for that first show were our friends, and friends of friends, including our Fiorucci sales assistant, Suzie. We had wheeled all of the clothes on a rolling rack into another tiny office where the models were to dress. The models started to arrive and do their own hair and makeup—something that is unheard of today.

Models in 1984 were not yet known as "supermodels." They were merely gorgeous women. All were individualists. These women were models by day, but were also leading independent, creative lives of their own as painters, photographers, filmmakers, and writers. These women made the clothes come alive with their own understanding of the role fashion plays in a woman's life, injecting their own personalities and life experiences into the presentation. They were like film actresses, really, with complex emotions and feelings toward the clothing they were about to present. They were responsible for communicating my vision to the audience.

As the show started, I held my breath. This was it! There was no holding back now. We were all so cramped in that tiny back room, there was hardly room to move. Since we had no idea how to organize a show, we didn't know about dressers—not that they would have fit anyway. Our enthusiastic models simply proceeded to help themselves to dresses that caught their eyes, in no particular order. All of them wore red tights and red plastic thong platform sandals that we had bought in Chinatown for a dollar a pair.

This was fashion as performance art. The first model carried the boom box out and placed it in the middle of the room. The collection included red, black, and white aerodynamic denim dresses and coats, as well as linen gaucho pants worn with flowing architectural duster coats. There were neat, clean shirtdresses with lantern sleeves, and linen opera coats with sleeves that I called "lid sleeves" worn over shorts and T-shirts.

The same elegant white gloves that
had served as invitations were
worn a few sizes too big on the
models' hands, making them
look a bit like Minnie and Mickey Mouse
for comic relief. Not that we
needed it—soon, the boom
box batteries were running
out and the wonderful
Cuban sound track started
to warp somewhere in the middle of the
presentation. As the music sagged, our lively
models proceeded to gently kick the boom box
into cooperating, much to the
audience's delight.

When the show
was over and the last
model popped backstage, I was
thrilled to hear the appreciative
applause. Not many people showed
up for our first show, but the ones who
did were the cream of the crop in the fashion
world: Dawn Mellow and Sydney Bachman
from Bergdorf Goodman, which was just across

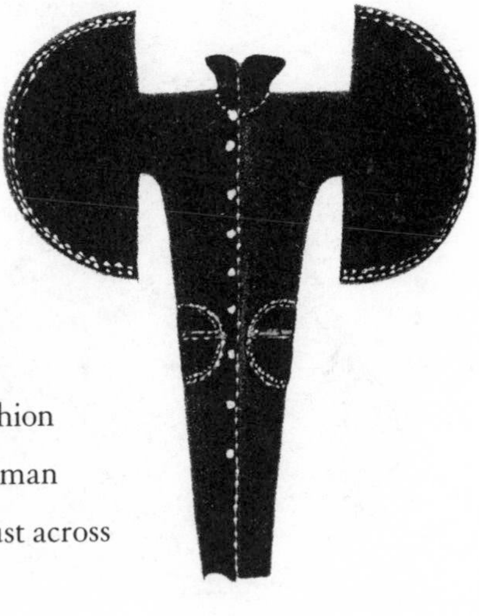

the street; Gene Pressman and Connie Darrow from Barneys New York; Bill Cunningham and Michael Gross from *The New York Times*; Kim Hastreiter from *Paper* magazine with our mutual friend Joey Arias; Annie Flanders and Ronnie Cook from *Details* magazine; and Polly Mellon and Jade Hobson from *Vogue* magazine.

Ruben and I were exhausted with joy. Together, we had officially brought the Isabel Toledo fashion label to life. Best of all, we had achieved the complex task of putting on a fashion show and we learned it all from start to finish by teaching ourselves the way to do it.

This kind of individuality grants you authenticity. What you do may not be perfect, but it can only be done by you.

New York City's magical fashion and art culture had made it possible for us to go into business for ourselves. It had provided the inspiration and energy for my first collection, and woven these gifted, talented people together and into my professional life.

8 Fueling a Self-Propelled Life

To succeed as an independent fashion designer,

you must stay nimble and trust your navigational

instincts.

JUST AS I NEVER IMAGINED THAT

I would become a fashion designer, once I

was a designer, I never could have predicted

the complex nature of fashion. I sensed going

into it that this was a tough business, and

that independent designers could succumb to the demands of the marketplace. I also discovered how competitive the fashion business can be, but I believe that fair competition is good. What I didn't realize was how many moving parts it takes to run the fashion machinery.

As a small design house, I had to learn to stay nimble, be flexible, and trust my navigational instincts in order not to get crushed. Fashion thrives on newness yet is oddly very set in its ways. Conservatism versus experimentation, innovation versus tradition: these ingredients are oddly complementary and part of what enriches the American fashion scene.

It is never smooth sailing, but creating in the gritty atmosphere of New York City has propelled me to design and develop a distinctive body of work that reflects the time from my particular vantage point. The diversity of fashion choices can come only from a varied climate, and New York City breeds some of the most diverse blooms found anywhere.

FUELING A SELF-PROPELLED LIFE

Ruben and I were off and running after that first exhausting, exhilarating fashion show. We quickly learned how to wear many different hats at once. This included arranging appointments to meet with store buyers, dealing with press and editorial requests from fashion magazines, placing production orders, and calling on new fabric vendors to start the process of designing the very next collection all over again. Through trial and error, we discovered how to juggle all of these different activities seamlessly.

Sometimes, it's a blessing when you have nothing to lose, and you can start your business on a shoestring. When you have no budget, you learn to create out of thin air. You also learn how to be conscientious. No throwaway thinking allowed! Pragmatism becomes your best friend, as you learn to do much with very little.

Mastering the smallest day-to-day details of running your business is the key to success. You can hire different people to do all of the different jobs, but the only way to truly understand how every piece of the business can be assembled into a well-oiled machine with a soul at its core is to do it all yourself. You must be your own boss, employee, intern, and mentor all at once. Ruben and I were lucky in this way: We could rely on each other to help carry this new load of responsibilities.

PLANTING NEW FASHION SEEDS

Meeting with fashion buyers from all of the different stores was an education all by itself. Now that I had received important press and attention from the industry, I was playing with the big kids on the fashion block.

The big names in fashion were in full assent, but the business landscape was still wide-open territory. The buyers from Bergdorf Goodman, Barneys, Saks, and Bloomingdale's were all competing for that elusive fashion customer who was brave enough to pioneer new looks.

There are always those few women who are on the lookout for a new designer with a different point of view. When women find a designer who cuts clothes that look good on their individual body types, and whose lifestyle and fashion suggestions gel with their own lives, a powerful wave is set in motion. This woman is an essential part of the fashion food chain, because she is open-minded and ready to adopt a new fashion that works for her. These designs are usually not yet ready for prime-time consumption. They are not yet popular, or even familiar-looking, yet this client takes a calculated risk.

You can't market to this woman because she goes by her instincts, discovering and feeling her way through the Grand Bazaar of Fashion. In the art world, you would call this woman a "patron of the arts"; in this case, she is collecting fashion. Sometimes, she may be young and just starting out in life. Or this woman may be very experienced, a woman who has seen and worn it all. The only thing for certain is that her fashion antennae are well tuned to her emotions. Her dressing and styling should not be confused with trendiness. In fact, it's the complete opposite: Sometimes her style picks will be years ahead of a trend. At other times, her style will never see the light of day anytime soon.

I adore this kind of individuality in fashion. It allows me to plant new fashion seeds in fertile style territories. This is what keeps fashion moving forward. Women who adopt a fashion and use it in their day-to-day lives are the perfect collaborators with designers. Fashion can't move ahead unless women set the wheels in motion by actually wearing new designs.

DEVELOPING A DESIGN ALPHABET

Great artists give form to their ideas through expert craftsmanship. At the Met, I had learned that each creator— whether in painting, sculpture, or fashion design—invents their own methods. In that way, an artist embeds her experiences and unique personality into the work itself. That is the artistic signature.

I had also discovered by now that an article of clothing is about much more than what you can see from the outside. Just as the designers whose work I had examined at the Met over the past four years had all developed their own personal alphabets and languages, I had been crafting the letters of my own design alphabet for many years, starting with that first tent dress in taupe linen that I topstitched as a child. Now, individual design letters were gradually becoming the words, sentences, and paragraphs of my story, which women would amplify by wearing my designs.

When I design, I often look at a part
of the body that has action. If I can play
with that action and maybe change the
silhouette, perhaps by draping cloth from
the bottom up instead of from the top
down, I can come up with something
unique. My early patterns—many of which
I call "action patterns" because of the way
they mimic the body's actions—developed
as I created ways to wrap fabric around the
body that weren't traditional. I was mainly
thinking about how to harness the body's
actions in a garment, while at the same
time giving the body maximum liberty,

as when I inserted jersey into the crotch of a pair of jeans or developed short sleeves that wouldn't show my armpits. Of course, I was still being informed by the fabrics I used as well, peering closely at the weave and pulling in different directions, cutting it to see how it collapsed, and so forth.

I like to feel the psychology of a garment, which may change as I wear it different ways. I never design collections according to any sort of theme. Many of my designs are spontaneous.

VOGUE COMES CALLING

While I was busy producing our first orders for stores, the fashion magazines were interested in writing stories and photographing the collections. We were thrilled to get a phone call from Grace Mirabella, the Editor-in-Chief of *Vogue*, to congratulate me on our first collection. She told us to expect a call from one of her talented fashion editors to arrange a meeting.

The very next day, Polly Mellen asked us to drop off some samples to be photographed by Steven Meisel for *Vogue* magazine. Polly was planning to write a fashion story on the "up and comers of 1986" and we were going to be included.

We showed up at a gritty loft on Broadway, which happened to be upstairs from Unique Clothing Warehouse, the very place where Ruben had worked just a few years before. Steven was easy to spot all over the Downtown scene, wearing his black fur hat even in summer, his eyes rimmed in dark kohl and his ever-ready camera dangling from a strap around his neck. Not only was my white denim car coat photographed that day, but Ruben and I were also cast into this fashion scene and captured in the Meisel composition as models in Steven's composition. The fact that Steven had once been a fashion illustrator made him a master photographer. He can spot a good line in the blink of an eye.

And, just like that, fashion's wide-open net scooped me up and caught me in its fascinating grip. Tuned-in fashion editors and journalists like Polly Mellen and Jade Hobson were the keepers of the fashion flame, responsible for spotting and shedding light on new fashion discoveries. The ability of these journalists to spot raw talent is an important part of the flow of fashion. Their instincts help nurture a healthy, promising fashion future creatively and economically, and they had the connection and resources to showcase fashion news. The rest would be up to us.

BECOMING PART OF THE GLOBAL FASHION COMMUNITY

Gradually, as more people began wearing my clothes, I had the thrill of passing strangers on the street who were wearing my designs. For example, soon after we began selling our clothing to stores, we saw a woman wearing an Isabel Toledo coat near Madison Square Garden. Ruben and I spotted the coat right away as the woman walked toward us, despite the fact that the city streets were in full rush-hour mode. That cozy, sculptural, cocoon-shaped camel coat, with its distinctive full lid sleeves, stood out to us in the crowd like a familiar friend. It all happened fast, in that New York City blur that is rush hour, yet the woman seemed to be moving toward us in slow motion.

We let her walk by without saying a word. We were in awe: Fashion fantasy had become reality. I felt proud, honored, and transformed by the realization that a woman had actually taken her hard-earned cash to Bergdorf Goodman—the brave store that had ordered this particular stand-out style— tried this coat on, and purchased it. It was a humbling and validating moment for me, knowing that I was of service to fashion and helping to dress women. I was now officially participating in the global fashion community.

I love this collaborative aspect of fashion. Fashion as a collective experience—as a public spectacle open to all who wish to add their voices and imprints to our time—is one of the most compelling aspects of this business for me. Women designers are in the unique position to not only come up with new design ideas, but to be active participants in the fashion parade that is time, because we can embody the idea itself. I can take a design idea out for test drives to fine-tune it to perfection before releasing it out into the world.

This thrill of experiencing my clothes being worn in real life, forming part of the collage of humanity, is still with me. Every time I pass someone wearing my clothes in any part of the world, it still moves me to think how lucky I am to be able to participate in the endless parade of fashion.

A STREAMLINED ME

Since I was so busy working and sewing, my life had to become as simplified and easy as possible. I was the opposite of a high-maintenance woman: I effortlessly adopted the concept of a closet for two and put to work my theory of a "streamlined me."

I wore my hair long and ponytailed and neatly stretched back and out of the way. By simplifying my look and my wardrobe, I left room to acquire

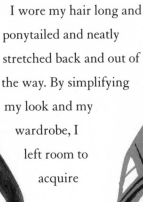

Ruben's. I also made room for my ever-growing body of new work. My daily uniform was based on a plain black turtleneck Capezio bodysuit worn with long, full, circular skirts cinched in at the waist with a tight leather belt. If I wasn't in the mood for a skirt, I substituted my always-faithful Levi's.

In the dead of winter, I wore skirts that were blanket-weight. I also layered tights over each other and then cut off the feet, creating my own leggings, as they hadn't been invented. I did this with several different-colored tights, and the effect was striking enough to not warrant much more fashion meddling. Too much fashion is a distraction sometimes.

For accessories, I wore gold hoop earrings, which completed the look of an existentialist Bohemian city dweller. Sometimes your look is a result of a necessary reality. My reality at this time was about keeping things as sharp, clear and simple as possible. Red lipstick and a compact were all I needed to get ready to step out.

TURNING TRASH INTO GOLD

By now, we had moved into our 42nd Street studio just off Times Square. We were directly across from a place called Peepland, surrounded by a number of other porn palaces, and above the world famous Nathan's Hot Dogs. Our rent was a whopping seventy-five dollars a month, which we split with our friend Benjamin Liu.

Benjamin was better known by many as Ming Vase, one of Andy Warhol's muses and trusted right-hand man. Like so many other New York artists we knew during that exciting time, he was involved in a staggering number of creative projects. It was Benjamin who helped spread the word about my first fashion show, convincing people that it would be worthwhile to attend.

Through Benjamin, we were invited to participate in a paper fashion show. I made a giant paper wedding dress for it using enormous sheets of white paper corded together in layers; Ruben helped me turn the paper into lace by using a hole puncher. The dress ended up being so enormous that we had to walk it down the street, since we couldn't fit it in a car; Andy Warhol bought it for his collection.

In his role as Andy Warhol's trusted assistant, Benjamin would often take Andy out on the town to see new places and meet new faces. This was how we ended up on Andy Warhol's cable TV show, *15 Minutes*, which was years ahead of its time. This was a truly unscripted reality show full of people who needed no script or direction in life; all Andy needed to do was turn on the lights, switch on the mic, and let the camera roll.

Our Andy Warhol interview segment was introduced by the great and enigmatic artist and photographer Peter Beard, who swung on a kid's schoolyard swing suspended from the high ceiling as he spoke into the camera. Ruben and I then interviewed each other, with Ruben asking most of the questions. We spoke in Spanish and English subtitles were added later on. The interview consisted of questions about art and fashion and the tug of war between the two, as well as our love affair. It was all done in fifteen minutes or less, but I'm so glad to know that the moment was captured forever, and delighted that Benjamin Liu prodded us to stop working long enough to pop in and be filmed by Don Munroe, the genius behind the lens of this cable TV time capsule.

Meanwhile, back at our studio just off of Times Square, I

worked diligently to make it as welcoming as possible. It was
about as gritty a space as you could get, even in New York.
Our studio was on the third floor and had been a former blood
bank. The previous tenant had left behind chocolate brown
vinyl recliners—where people used to sit to have their blood
drawn—and large glass industrial refrigerators, since they
were too large and heavy to move.

I love the challenge of designing spaces to create peace
and order. I'm constantly moving things around in a work
space until the energy feels right. In our 42nd Street studio, I
scrubbed the walls and refrigerators until they gleamed, and
discovered that the refrigerators were perfect for storing fabric
and tools, paintbrushes and paper. I filled the giant windows
with geraniums that happily grew to over six feet tall. The
scarlet blooms framed the bustling, vibrant street scene of 42nd
Street, where the giant blinking eyeball peeping through a
keyhole at the Peepland Emporium across the street became
the visual symbol for us of a New York City that has long since
disappeared.

Our studio door had a bullet hole that you could peer
through to see if we were home. It opened and closed on a
single hinge, and it was missing a doorknob, so we kept the
door closed with a bicycle chain and lock. But no worries about
security, since the cheap rents soon attracted other artists like

Mike Bidlo, Bruno Schmidt, Jack Pierson, and photographer
Todd Eberle. It was soon all in the family. This address became
a sort of *Salon des Refusés*.

While scary and menacing to traverse, this block provided
a haven for young artists, writers, and photographers just
starting out, giving us a foothold and helping us crack open the
doors to our future. It's no wonder that some of the best scenes
in the movie *Slaves of New York* based on Tama Janowitz's
book were filmed in these studios. This was an artist colony in
the midst of New York City's hustle and bustle.

To this dubious headquarters came not only our trusting
buyers, who now included the amazing duo of Gene Pressman
and Connie Darrow from Barneys New York, but also the
Fendi sisters, who were in town to research artists to work
with them on the opening day of their new Fifth Avenue store.
Valerie Steele was brave enough to make an appointment
to come and see me there as part of her research for her
upcoming book *Women in Fashion*.

One day, Kim Hastreiter surprised us by popping in with
movie director Pedro Almodovar, who was in town to premiere
his latest movie, *Tie Me Up, Tie Me Down*. Pedro asked me
to make up some flamenco dresses for three up-and-coming
starlets of New York City life—RuPaul, Lady Bunny, and La
Homma—to wear to the movie premiere.

Hip-hop historian, musician, and artist extraordinaire Fab Five Freddy and photographer Ron Galella also filed through, working on different projects. Ron, who is perhaps the most famous true paparazzo of our time due to his photo reportage on Jackie Onassis, did a magnificent spoof of himself stalking designers and fashion models throughout the city.

Ron's photo of the model Dovana, which he took while she was wearing my giant silk chiffon pony skin skirt, still makes me smile: She is standing over a grate on Times Square and letting the rush of air from the subway cars blow the skirt up around her legs. Dovana looks like a dark-haired pixie-cut Beatnik Marilyn Monroe in that picture, and this image somehow encapsulates that time and environment perfectly.

GOING WITH THE FLOW

I tried not to read reviews, but I was honored when Ruben showed me an article by Hebe Dorsey in the *International Herald Tribune*, where I was included as part of a "new wave" in international fashion with John Galliano, Romeo Gigli, and Marc Jacobs in a list of designers described as "ready to take risks" and "seriously interested in couture."

Naturally, good reviews brought us more business and created

fresh challenges. One of the biggest hurdles we faced initially was
having enough space to work. Finding a place to work where
you can thrive and feel creative is essential if you're going to reach
your potential as an artist, but it is never easy, especially in an
ever-changing city like New York. Nothing is permanent here,
so you have to follow your hunches. We migrated with the flow
of the city's energy. And, in tune with our artist antennae, we
went wherever time stood still and the economy forgot.

Ruben and I soon found ourselves feeling too crowded in
Times Square. We were both growing and needed space, and
my production had taken over the Blood Bank, which is what
we lovingly called "the 42nd Studio."

Since we are both walkers, preferring that method of
transportation over any other, we had a pretty good sense of
where we could find more space for the lowest possible price.
We both loved the architecture of a modular, curved, brick
colossus of a building way over on 12th Avenue called The
Lehigh Building. We had walked past it many times, since the
only place you could park your car for free was on the deserted
piers along the Hudson River.

In life, rewards seldom come your way without fringe
annoyances, and this area had plenty. The Lehigh Building—
now known as the Starrett-Lehigh Building—was on the far
West Side, and this location was a bit brutal in every way. Its

most challenging aspect was the nearly overwhelming stench of the nearby meat market, especially in the summer. But it was gorgeous at the end of the day to see the sunset over New Jersey, and to smell the ocean creeping up the Hudson.

A classic Art Deco design, the Lehigh Building was a streamlined industrial wonder that featured an elevator for trucks that could load and unload cargo all the way up to its top floors. Long neglected due to the decrease in New York City's manufacturing scene, its block-long hallways were more like avenues, and usually so deserted that you could hear the echo of your own footsteps. We easily found a 7,000-square-foot space available for rent.

We had the nerve to offer a thousand dollars a month for it. This might sound like a steal now, but it was a huge financial risk for us then. Luckily, the building was managed by none other than Leona Helmsley, who must have had a soft spot for art and fashion, because she consented to our offer.

Our new space was vast and glorious, with *Star Trek*–like columns forming a continuous ribbon of V-shaped cement divisions. It not only provided Ruben with enough space to stretch larger paintings and make bigger sculptures and installations, but also gave me the room I needed to add another sewing machine and cutting table. In fact, the studio was so large that we even had the opportunity to hold our second fashion show there.

Since I had been lucky enough to receive such great press coverage by *The New York Times*, *Harper's Bazaar*, *Elle*, *Vogue*, and other fashion publications, we were overwhelmed by show ticket requests this time around. We enlisted Benjamin Liu to help us organize that show and others in the future.

For this production, we snaked chairs in a single unbroken row throughout the entire space, so that everyone had the opportunity to have a front row seat. Ruth Finley, who organized the Fashion Calendar, called us up to suggest that we list our fashion show's date, time, and location with her. The Fashion Calendar held all of Fashion Week together, especially back then, when there were no organized tents yet. Every designer simply picked a place that would reflect the mood of a particular collection, trying to choose the environment that would best define his or her fashion vision for the season. This meant traveling all around town on a wild-goose chase to find the next show's location. Ruth had the unenviable job of working with each designer to book the shows near enough to each other so that the fashion flock had a chance to arrive on time to each show.

Photographer Bill Cunningham was usually the man we all waited for to arrive before starting the show. Since he pedaled on his bike instead of catching a ride in a car, you could generally assume that anyone who was going to come was already in the house by the time you saw him appear.

We had no formal seating arrangement. It was first come, first served—a custom we always tried to maintain while we held runway shows. This guaranteed a wonderfully unexpected and very democratic mix of people. An important fashion journalist might find himself sitting next to a drag performer, a museum curator might be seated beside a textile manufacturer, and so forth. This gave the audience a fresh vibrancy, putting them in an enthusiastic mood for what was to come.

I have always welcomed audience participation in my
shows. A fashion show is a performance. The models feed on
the energy of the public and bring this with them backstage.
I can always tell if a collection is being well received by the
looks on the models' faces and by their energy level during a
show. Your very first review as a designer is from the models'
reactions.

Another important difference between our first and second
fashion shows was the participation of Audrey Smaltz and The
Ground Crew. We had met Audrey at a fashion event where I
was a participant. I'm a lover of organization and clear-headed
planning. Audrey is a master of organizing the backstage
machinery of a fashion show. When she is involved, every detail
is choreographed, right down to the racks and dressers being
there to help the models get in and out of their clothes in split
seconds. Audrey was generous and kind, and she and her crew
knew how to create a master game plan, double-check it, and
carry it through. We counted on her for many shows after that.

After another exhausting but exhilarating show season, it
was back to the reality of production. I quickly learned that
our new space, which was nowhere near a subway line and
too long a walk through dark, deserted streets inhabited by
prostitutes and their dubious clients, was less than ideal. We
couldn't get any seamstresses to work with us, because we

couldn't convince them to travel off the well-beaten path of Seventh Avenue to get to our streamlined fashion hub.

Once again, the hunt was on for the perfect place to live and work.

AFTER ALL OF THE DECAYING industrial glamour of the Lehigh Building, I was yearning for sunlight and water. Since we had a car and could drive in and out of Manhattan, we migrated out toward Coney Island.

It wasn't long before we found a really low-cost, nature-inspired solution to our studio dilemma. Our new space was just a block from the Atlantic Ocean, and it was heaven to take breaks between sewing marathons and go for a swim with Ruben. In the winter, this habit was replaced by long, brisk walks along the Coney Island boardwalk, where the only people besides Ruben and me were the Russian senior citizens huddled together on the benches. Clad in their magnificent furs, they took in the winter sun, wearing very little beneath their coats and capes so that they could open them up and let the sun warm their skin.

It didn't take long, however, for us to tire of the constant commuting in and out of Manhattan for appointments and deliveries. It didn't help that our old car was slowly giving out, either. The final straw was when the car overheated in the middle of the Brooklyn Bridge on an ultra-hot summer day, and had to be pushed along by a friendly policeman in his car with flashing lights.

After having circled Manhattan from both the west, via the Lincoln Tunnel, and the east, crossing the romantic Brooklyn Bridge, we could no longer deny the importance of being in New York City to experience a cosmopolitan life. This city gave us what it takes to make it in a global environment.

We gave up our place on Coney Island when we found a fantastic loft right in Midtown. In the age-old tradition of the Ma and Pa business model, we made it a point to live and work in the same space, affording us the luxury to waste no time on commuting—quite a green concept, if I say so myself.

JAPAN TO THE RESCUE

As the economy on Wall Street started to take a nosedive in the late 1980s, Ruben and I experienced a steady and frightening decline in our revenue. American buyers, both big and small, were tightening their belts. Retail buyers' budgets were being severely cut, and the first fashion lines to go were usually the younger, less-established fashion ones like mine.

Fortunately for us, as the United States experienced a steep decline, other countries were still on the upswing and had enough fashion dollars to spend on American talent. We had the opportunity to go where the grass was greener. There was always a green patch somewhere. This seems to be a downside of today's globalization where we are all so intertwined. The beauty of choices and differences is essential to the spark of creativity. Out of chaos, much beauty can emerge.

Interest in American style was particularly strong in Japan at that time. Ruben had been drawing his fashion satire cartoons in the back page of *Details* magazine since meeting Annie Flanders at one of my fashion shows. Annie had shown so much enthusiasm for his drawings that she offered Ruben the back page to do whatever he thought might work for the magazine's audience. Ruben's idea was to do political satires on the fashion world he encountered, with all of its unique participants. These drawings had become well known and widely collected, especially in Japan.

Given Ruben's dedicated Japanese following, it wasn't long before I was discovered in Japan, too. I was invited to create a special collection made entirely of antique kimono textiles to celebrate the century anniversary of this industry. These fabrics are all hand-dyed, using an ancient technique relying on a type of mushroom that produces a very intense shade of indigo.

The clothing that I chose to design was inspired by the many techniques these talented craftspeople used to create an infinite variety of textiles, from dyed cotton velvets as lush as fur, to gossamer-thin linens as delicate as spiderwebs. My favorite is a tatami-like cotton weave that I still continue to use in one form or another.

I broke ground with that collection and let myself go with more experimental designs, using much more yardage than I ever could have afforded without this sponsorship. This is when I began my many experiments with the manipulation of fabrics, gathering them, twisting them, and redirecting them in new and surprising directions. Many of the designs were based on my packable shapes. These garments would fold flat like a kimono, but had the wonderful fluidity of the curved, tailored line. I loved exploring how these two schools of thought merged in clothing construction, and described these new designs as "East Meets West."

We showed the collection first in Tokyo, and I fell in love with Japan at once. I admire the scale of things in Japan, the people, and its many green spaces. As a city gardener myself, I especially love seeing how the Japanese manage to create gardens out of any space available. Even if you have three feet of terrace in Japan, it seems, you will find a garden growing there.

After stopping in Tokyo, Ruben and I traveled south to Tokushima, where I was given the keys to this city in the central indigo-producing region of Japan. This magical city by the ocean had palm trees lining its main avenues and pine trees on its side streets. You can always tell which way you're headed by the trees even if you're a visitor—a brilliant and ancient form of city planning. Another incredible feature of that lovely city is that the dedicated people who work with this indigo cloth in Tokushima all have their hands permanently tinted a beautiful shade of blue.

THIS WONDERFUL TRIP TO JAPAN was the first of many for us. Ruben had appeared in the ad campaign for Parco department stores in the early 1980s when he had been drawn by the great fashion illustrator Pater Sato for their men's fashion campaign. You can imagine the honor Ruben felt ten years later when he was asked to hold an exhibition of his own drawings, paintings, and illustrations at Parco Galleries, located inside the fashion megastore in Tokyo.

Both Parco and Seibu were now carrying my collections as well. It was an exhilarating experience to travel to Japan and see women wearing my clothes and styling them to suit their lives in Tokyo, which had become one of the most style-forward capitals in the world as Japan emerged in the 1980s to become an important fashion incubator. I was impressed by the way the Tokyo women effortlessly mixed my more abstract and formal pieces with track shorts and sneakers to wear to work in the daytime. I also admired the way they layered my dresses and topped them off with shiny baseball jackets two sizes too big.

This was the start of the Japanese fashion pinball game later described as "Harajuku girl dressing," a way of bouncing things off each other that don't necessarily go together, making a collage of your wardrobe for a highly personal look. It was a visual delight and an exploration of consumerism embraced to the fullest. It is always fascinating to witness another point of view, another take on the age-old ritual of fashion.

SEVENTH AVENUE OPERA

Another important Japanese project that Ruben and I had the opportunity to collaborate on took place in Kobe. Ruben was commissioned to dream up and produce an opening event for a fashion hall and museum being constructed there. After much deliberation, we decided that he would invent what we called "The Seventh Avenue Opera." This would include a fashion show by several American designers selected by Ms. Junko

Oishi and The Kobe Fashion Museum. The designers included Todd Oldham, Zang Toi, and—luckily for me—Isabel Toledo! This was to be a huge affair, and an artistic project on the biggest scale we had ever tackled thus far.

For this undertaking, Ruben enlisted the help of our friend Juan Ramos, who had been the creative partner of the legendary fashion artist Antonio Lopez. The collaborations of these two brilliant men in the fashion world reached back to the mid-1960s. Together, they had revolutionized fashion illustration both in the U.S. and in Europe, often collaborating with the great designer Charles James, and both knew the fashion world like the back of their hand.

We first met Juan after he attended one of my early fashion shows, and got to know him very well after Antonio passed away. He had come to the U.S. from Puerto Rico as a child, majored in interior design at FIT, and became a multifaceted art director. Like Mrs. Vreeland at the Met, he was inspired and inspiring to talk to about fashion, and was always generous about sharing his store of wide-ranging information. People like Juan and Mrs. Vreeland are national living treasures and vital to moving fashion forward because of their firsthand knowledge and serious interest in the art forms of fashion.

We became instant family, meeting Juan several times a week for coffee and meals. Juan loved coffee shops and

diners. After living with Antonio in Paris, he had really
gained an appreciation for all things American, including
the kinds of casual diners and coffee shops still found on
almost every corner of New York City. These proved to be the
perfect inexpensive, casual places to hold our weekly talking
marathons and creative debates.

After hours of discussion about my design methods, Juan
was the first to describe my work with jersey as "liquid
architecture." He was also the first person to suggest that I
really should be showing my collections in Paris, because they
would be more appreciated there. That advice I would follow
soon enough, when the opportunity presented itself.

For the Kobe show, Ruben designed and painted the sets
for the atrium of this new complex. He made it look like our
old and beloved Times Square by painting giant surrealistic
fashion ads and billboards. Some paintings were as tall as a
four-story building. One billboard was designed to flip over to
show animated films that Ruben had made to announce each
designer's show. At one point, the set was filled with dancers
pushing garment racks in every direction, while models
walked through and cleared the way to create the runway.

The whole performance was really an homage to the great
big Seventh Avenue fashion machine, complete with all of
its characters. We engaged our friend Joey Arias to be the

Master of Ceremonies, and I designed all of Joey's costumes for each segment of the show. These included a giant New York City cockroach tuxedo look, complete with transparent brown wings and a top hat—a sort of New York City Mayor of the Underground look.

For this show, each designer's segment was also punctuated by a dance performance by the brilliant Doug Elkins Dance Company. Their interpretation of a disco square dance meets a ballet tango performed on point by the male and female members was a riveting and energizing scene. I find the relationships between movement, choreography and the emotional relationship to fashion as a source of constant inspiration. A body in movement, and the way cloth mimics and echoes these movements, are fuel for the imagination, and can jump-start an entire new collection for me.

THE NEW BOHEMIANS

The fluid New York fashion scene was changing once again. There was a sense of a Downtown versus Uptown aesthetic battle. The younger design names all seemed to be clumped together as Downtown designers no matter where we really came from. Somehow, this seemed to imply a not-ready-for-mass-consumption point of view.

The Uptown aesthetic was certainly more tied in with Wall Street and the economy. The look had more of a "let them eat cake" mentality and sensibility. Uptown had always catered to the Ladies Who Lunch, while my clothes were more for those who like a good picnic.

Sometimes this friction is good for creativity. It makes designers try harder or continue to differentiate themselves further. It is certainly a good thing when women have plenty of well-defined choices to try out when it comes to getting dressed. Too much sameness leads to apathy and boredom, which is never good for business.

In the late eighties, my work was all about introducing a new Bohemianism into the fashion vocabulary. I was striving to create expressions of calligraphy in cloth; I wanted to capture the act of drawing with ink on paper and mimic the effortless flow of the gestures I saw in Ruben's illustration.

My newest creations emerged from my sewing machine as drippy black dresses in soft, very female silhouettes. I began to wash silk satins, silk faille, and silk gazar. These fabrics were all best known in the grand tradition of the Parisian couture. Now I wanted to extract the ingredient of the unapproachable and remove the aspect of the snooty by washing away the formal nature of the fabrics and injecting an element of American casual into them.

My aim here was to create user-friendly yet imposing architecture. I was taking off from where the French couture houses had stopped many years before, attempting to reintroduce high fashion concepts from an American sensibility.

Fashion is a continuous dialogue among artists, designers, countries, cultures, and even across time. When the haute couture tradition seemed exhausted and irrelevant by the early 1970s, fashion was revitalized by ready-to-wear garments, specifically by the American sportswear point of view. The haute couture culture was still turning out masterpiece dressmaking, but it seemed disconnected and too prissy for most modern lifestyles. Ready-to-wear had replaced couture, but it was American sportswear that had placed the direct style power on women. Fashion was now open to interpretation and it became much more casual in spirit.

By the late 1980s, however, the American sportswear attitude was rapidly losing steam. It seemed too sloppy and low impact; somehow, it had lost its emotional connection to women by becoming too familiar. The ever-expanding fashion industry had given us so many versions of the same look that it had become too watered down. For me, couture held the secrets of workmanship and craft that had first intrigued me during my internship days at the Met. If I felt this way, I was certain that other women did, too.

All of this experimentation was evident in my collections. I was proposing the antidote to the 1980s power suit and power dressing, which by now had solidified into the corporate Wall Street uniform. The big hair and big shoulders of the 1980s were starting to deflate because the economy's downturn had pulled the plug on that party.

While the economy continued to sour, our business in New York was being stripped down to its bare bones. The slow economy encouraged venues around town to become more user-friendly. I was now showing my collections in some very interesting free spaces, including forgotten architectural gems like Number 2 Columbus Circle, which we called "The Cheese Building."

The exterior skin of this building, which is now home to the Museum of Art and Design, was wrapped in circular portals, a design that let in the light. The circular motif was perfect for my design vocabulary, gelling seamlessly with my preferred pattern shapes. The models wore bubble-shaped ponytails that echoed the Swiss cheese holes of the architecture.

Business was so bad all over town that restaurants, bars, and nightclubs were eager to generate the free publicity and to get fashion people in their door. As long as we could book an early daytime slot with Ruth at the Fashion Calendar, most places made themselves available. This free-form, fluid collaboration among artists, designers, and businesspeople in New York City is part of the energetic and vibrant weave not easily found elsewhere in the world.

In addition to the Cheese Building, I also showed collections in some of the same places where Ruben and I had once gone dancing, then later earned money by doing art projects when we were first starting out. Places like Limelight, The Supper Club, and the Palladium opened their doors to me, as did The Underground, which was downstairs from Andy's old *Interview* magazine office on Union Square. I showed at Xenon and Studio 54, which had reopened under all new management but was now just a shadow of its former glamorous self. The entire city had lost a bit of its surefire glitz. The gold leaf was fading, and so were the budgets for buyers.

"Their open to buy" was consistently cut back season after season, despite the fact that my clothes were still selling. So, when our friends from *Visionaire* magazine invited us to join them in Paris, we decided to buy some show trunks, pack up our collection, and take our show on the road. The voice of our friend Juan Ramos urging us to bring my collection to Paris was ringing in my ears. His advice to go show in Paris could not have been better.

FASHION MECCA, HERE WE COME: OUR FIRST SHOW IN PARIS

With the help of our friends Stephen Gan, James Kaliardos, and Cecilia Dean, who had all recently founded the magazine *Visionaire*, we headed to Paris with two trunks full of my latest collection. We had met Stephen when he worked as a fashion editor for *Details* magazine. Since Ruben

had been drawing the last page of that
magazine until Annie Flanders sold it
to Condé Nast, we had become very
close to "the *Visionaire* kids," as we
called them.

James Kaliardos had collaborated
with me on makeup for many of my
shows early on, which was anything but
subtle. The makeup sometimes featured blooming flowers and
leaves for the eyes, fruit-smudged lips instead of lipstick, and eye
shadow drawn on to resemble the women in Ruben's drawings
and cartoons for *Details*. His inspired hand transformed the
models into a pack of glamorous raccoons and black-eyed peas
for the autumn collection I was about to show in Paris.

These friends invited us to camp out
with them in a huge apartment. We
experienced Paris as a fantastic
sprawling medieval village
transformed by modern times.
It seemed like an adult Walt
Disney kingdom, with the
different districts all connected
by marvelous winding
boulevards.

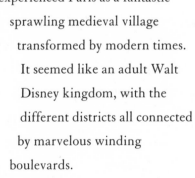

Since Ruben and I were on a tight budget, we walked everywhere, traversing Paris from one corner to the other. We walked for hours at a time between business appointments and meals with friends. That is the best way to get to know a city: Walk it from corner to corner. This was also a necessity for us in Paris, because the subway trains all closed down around midnight. If New York is the city that never sleeps, Paris was the opposite, and stubbornly so.

Most taxi drivers also seemed to be very fond of a good night's sleep. Even if you *could* find a taxi, the driver would surely be in a nasty mood and not headed where you wanted to go. But if you did manage to find a taxi, chances are they could point out which way the Chanel headquarters were, where the Dior and Hermès shops were, or how to get to La Samaritaine, a department store where you could buy old-fashioned French workers' clothes.

We soon found out that Paris is the city where

all people speak fashion fluently. Style and craft

are held in ultra-high esteem in that city,

second only to the appreciation for art

and the artist. Paris loves fashion, and

fashion loves Paris. The twice-yearly

ready-to-wear collections

held in the

city are

like global

conventions

for the

appreciation

of female

beauty,

workmanship, and all of the glamour and prestige associated with that.

JUAN RAMOS HAD RECOMMENDED THAT we see his old friend, fashion publicist Sylvie Grumbach, the minute we set foot in Paris. She agreed to meet us at an outdoor café to discuss the arrangements; we had a most delicious beer with our breakfast there to cinch the deal: Sylvie lent us her organizational expertise, and her professional staff set up the show.

With Sylvie, we witnessed for the first time the kind of protective care that Paris gives to artistic creations. She and her assistant guarded my collection after the show like two stone lionesses, only allowing certain journalists to sneak a peek and touch the textiles.

In Paris, we were also privileged to meet the legendary model Bettina Graziani, who still carries the torch for Parisian elegance. Bettina may be one of the world's first supermodels, helping to inspire and define decades of French fashion design through her generous personality, humanity, and instinctive intelligence. From Hubert de Givenchy to Azzedine Alaïa, Bettina is the elegant thread that ties together the last sixty years of French fashion and style. She continues to inspire and support fashion culture. We were thrilled to see her at our first show in Paris, sitting front and center.

We held that show in a tiny café hidden on a crooked street off the Bastille. The designer Franck Joseph Bastille had found us the café to host the very first show; his atelier was just upstairs in the attic, which would be convenient for dressing and changing the models. Franck had become well known for his wonderfully inspired embroideries, like furry rats running across skirt hems, or oil-slicked lobsters inspired by the River Seine.

Franck had a great sense of humor. He took us on historical walking tours late into the night, talking about the legends of medieval Paris, the catacombs below the streets, and the layers of history hiding in plain sight. These layers are much easier to see at night, when all is deserted. Meanwhile, he made us laugh with his very contemporary gossip about the Parisian fashion world.

OUR FIRST SHOW IN PARIS was surprisingly well attended, packing the tiny café to capacity. This collection included jersey trousers with narrow leather suspenders that the models wore with lace tops. I also made a series of long matte jersey dresses in red and black, and the models wore masks that looked like veils.

During the show, the models had to walk up and down five flights of winding stairs to get to the attic atelier. They were very good sports about it and never missed a beat. When they finally reached the bottom of the stairs, they had to traverse an alleyway and courtyard in the rain to enter the café from the back. The audience couldn't have been more attentive or appreciative, and most of the people who attended that first Paris fashion show are still our friends to this day.

Among the guests was fashion designer extraordinaire Adeline André, who brought Bettina with her. We also met the fashion scholar and historian Florence Muller, who was then the curator of the Musée de la Mode et du Textile, and her husband, artist Goran Vejvoda, who would go on to supply the musical sound track for many of my future shows.

After the Paris show, we headed back to New York and did it all over again. We kept up this back-and-forth between Paris and New York for several years. It was double the work, but a huge learning experience. Travel is an excellent way to broaden your perspective and learn valuable lessons in how others interpret your work.

My collections in Paris were very well received. It was curious, actually, to see how I wasn't perceived as an American designer in Europe. Instead, the foreign press and buyers saw me as a Spanish designer, preferring somehow to link me to that country. Others considered me a Cuban designer; Cuba was still shrouded in mystery, because so few people had been allowed in to Cuba for so many years.

Showing in both New York and Paris allowed me to stay

afloat financially. I managed to sell to some international accounts, while at the same time strengthening my New York City business base. The economy was finally recovering, at least at the Toledo house.

IF YOU GET UNDERSTOOD TOO EARLY, MAYBE YOU'VE SAID IT ALL

By this time, my accidental career had morphed into a full-fledged business. Since Ruben and I have always been self-propelled, we have always taken turns at the wheel, navigating our way around the shifting sands of the fashion business and adapting to many new circumstances.

By now, Ruben and I had been in business for over ten years. We had learned to survive by taking turns at the wheel. When my business was slow, Ruben would take on more commercial work. He has always considered himself a combination artist and journalist. His training at *Details* magazine served him well, because he had to turn drawings in on tight deadlines—sometimes even overnight. Ruben does thrive on deadlines, which is perfect for the endless treadmill of fashion. On the other hand, whenever my business was strong, Ruben could drift into his own artwork without the intrusion of time, which in turn fuels my fashion design work. This organic cycle was not planned out, but we sure were lucky to find it. It is the most productive and seamless way to achieve much inspired work.

Our House of the Self-Taught continued to explore different expressions in dressing. I had moved on from my elementary stage, which had been all about creating kitelike pattern shapes that resembled bold, graphic, line-stitched drawings. I had entered a more Bohemian stage in my work, transforming those original graphic kite shapes into sensual, Calder-like mobiles. I explored these techniques, coining the term "liquid architecture" along the way.

The collapsing of all of these bold pattern shapes into such mysteriously fragile clothes proved to be very user-friendly and was readily accepted at the retail level. These clothes were easy to wear, but full of magical realism. This experimentation in draping led to what I called "suspension," and, eventually, to "organic geometry." My draping mathematical equations inspired me to push farther and farther in this direction, only to again search out the drawn line.

This time I found that drawn line in lace. Lace has the ability to lead a double life, at once fragile and mysteriously strong in its seductive weave. It came to be known in my House as "shadow," an element that I return to again and again, and one that would play such an important part in creating the right dress for First Lady Michelle Obama on her husband's Inauguration Day. Using lace as a component in my designs continues to intrigue me, always inspiring me to investigate its emotional properties.

THE SHOWS STOP HERE

In 1998, after many years of holding runway presentations, I stopped showing and decided to be silent and continue my exploration in a private environment. There were a number of reasons for this.

By the late 1990s, the quaint and intimate persona of fashion had begun a fast-paced growth into what we know today as the megabrands. The days when fashion designers were expected to propose new ideas and solutions for dressing women had shifted to an era of branding. The fashion machinery had become too expensive for me to continue participating in the show cycle.

The fashion cycle had swung in another direction. The idea that designers should be encouraged to explore raw concepts and take creative risks was almost extinct, because it was seen as too financially risky. The fashion scene shifted to the entertaining, slick theatrical productions of the fashion shows themselves. The emphasis was no longer on the clothes; in fact, the spotlight seemed to be on everything *but* the clothes. Accessories became the main focus, because that was where the profit was made, and clothes formed merely a backdrop to sell accessories.

This may have been a reasonable business formula at the time, but women were left unsatisfied. This shift was not bad for my business, because it left buyers craving good and rare fashions for their most discerning clients. However, it created a dismal climate for the culture of fashion itself, which thrives on seasonal innovations to generate excitement and keep moving fashion forward. If there are no real clothes to lust over, our fashion audience starts to lose interest.

Our buyers continued to place orders, and our private clients continued to show interest in my designs and to order their wardrobes each season. My voice may have been silent, but the strength of my work continued to communicate and, in a way, perhaps my message was even stronger.

Today, with the fashion world's corporate race to expand businesses to be bigger and bigger, the quest for guessing the "right" fashion answers becomes everyone's leading concern. Designing by consensus becomes the new standard, and puts the individual voices of creators at risk. Designing minds need time to nurture original ideas and allow them to develop. This is like replanting a forest: If we don't allow enough time for this important natural process, we end up with open ground that is barren of new ideas.

The saving grace of the ever-swinging fashion pendulum and the fashion business structure itself is its ability to shed its carcass over and over again to find a new expression, yet hopefully never at the risk of the artistry of fashion.

9 Rising Above

When you're an artist, there is no map to tell you
which way to fly or safety net to catch you. Art
is about discovery, invention, and the way you
define your vision.

WHEN YOU'RE AN ARTIST, YOU
have no map to show you the right
direction or safety net to catch you when
you fall. You have to find your own vision
through discovery, passion, and intuition.

My bliss lies in continually experimenting and discovering new territories.

Evolving a thought or an emotion into something real and practical is a constant challenge. Transforming the abstract and intangible ingredient to the pragmatic solution is my reward. Over time, I have learned my craft in this way. Now I can bend the rules further and inject all I have discovered into the commercial.

FALLING OFF THE FASHION TREADMILL

By the late 1990s, I could feel the industry change. The intimate and personal nature of high fashion had begun speedily transforming into what we have today: a market defined by megabrands. As fashion becomes more accessible and easily digested by all, it risks becoming overly familiar. Or, perhaps even worse, trivial.

We can't blame the big brands for this expansion, because it seems like the media and we, the fashion-conscious public, can't get enough of them. But on the other hand, too much familiarity can diffuse the allure. This attraction-repulsion syndrome is like the push-pull between love and hate, where a thin thread separates the two.

As an independent designer, I saw this moment as clearly as writing on a wall. The fashion business was revving up on Botox and the excitement level had to be pumped up a few notches. The era of fashion as an entertainment and media event on a grand scale was about to begin. This is an expensive proposition, one that requires deep pockets and a different concept of what clothes are for.

One thing was clear: I could not invest in this kind of venture. My resources and focus must all go into the development and make of the clothes themselves. My staff and my craft are always my focus. The media aspect, as important and creative as that can be, was way out of my game plan at the time.

There is nothing worse than feeling like you're spinning your wheels and going nowhere in business. If you listen to your instincts, you can always save yourself from this distraction. All it takes is remaining open to working things out in your own way. I decided to step off the fashion treadmill in the nick of time, before the speed accelerated.

Of course, by not staging runway shows, I risked becoming invisible. Our well-meaning fashion friends advised us to keep showing, to pay attention to our packaging, and to hire a press agent. They were afraid that my voice wouldn't be heard if I didn't show during Fashion Week.

I knew that they might be correct. But I wanted to

somehow maintain the essence of the personal in fashion. The intimacy of fashion was what had always inspired me and attracted me to design. I knew that women like to discover things for themselves and come to their own conclusions in their fashion choices.

The great thing about the American fashion scene has always been its diversity. There is always room for choices. Our American sensibility means that we thrive on differences. American women have a rainbow of options, as wide open or as narrow and focused as they choose.

I sensed that women were not only willing, but eager to find clothing that was so far off the beaten track that it couldn't be on anyone's radar. This sense of the unexpected is a healthy component of fashion. The fact that the fashion business was growing into another, bigger version of itself actually left room in its underbelly for something new and gentler to develop.

I wanted to take time to look, to absorb, and to allow my designs to develop even more organically. I decided that there would be no more biannual runway shows for me. I would no longer partake in the Fashion Week cycle. Never had I been less interested in making clothes at breakneck speed. Just as I had after high school, I was ready to take a sabbatical of the soul and work at a pace more in keeping with my own internal rhythms.

SHARING MY LANGUAGE

Dr. Valerie Steele is a genius fashion historian and the author of books such as *Paris Fashion* and *Fifty Years of Fashion: New Look to Now* in 1997. She had interviewed me a decade before while researching her book, *Women of Fashion: Twentieth-Century Designers*. She had also become the director of The Museum at FIT.

I had developed an enormous respect for Valerie over the years as the two of us had followed our unique career paths. Since the late 1980s, Valerie has forged new ground on the examination of the social significance of fashion's impact on the culture at large. Her insights have been instrumental in fostering a view of fashion culture as something beyond it being just simple merchandise.

Consequently, when she approached me in 1997 and explained her idea of presenting an exhibit of my designs and Ruben's artwork together at FIT, we were both floored, especially when I realized that this would be FIT's first exhibit ever to highlight the creative work of a living American designer. I was honored beyond words by the realization that Valerie, one of the most knowledgeable fashion historians of our time, wanted to mount an exhibition of the work I'd done over the last fourteen years.

For the museum show, Valerie and I worked together to select about seventy of my garments, reaching back to pre-collection days, with some items even dating back to our time at Fiorucci. We also selected an equal number of Ruben's artworks to exhibit. These included paintings, sculptures, mannequins, and illustrations that directly linked back to my body of work, as a way of highlighting our collaboration.

The yin and yang of art and fashion was the meeting ground for this exhibit, titled, "Toledo/Toledo: A Marriage of Art and Fashion." Ruben's early satirical drawings for *Details* magazine were on display, as well as *The Sewing Machine*, a painting inspired by my love affair with that particular industrial tool.

We also featured a dozen or so of our many sketchbooks filled with an inventory of design ideas. Through Ruben's sketches, the public could see how he and I worked together to transform my ideas first into patterns, and then into three-dimensional articles of clothing. These sketchbooks were cracked open to show the quick shorthand gestures that captured the blueprints for my design ideas. Since I don't work from sketches, Ruben and I had developed this way of working in order to better communicate with our pattern makers and seamstresses. Our friends at *Visionaire* designed a book by the same title to accompany the exhibition. Since we had known them for so long and they were so intimate with our work, this book was an organic collaboration.

Our main goal was to create an exhibit that could clearly illustrate my design process, how clothes work, how pattern pieces fit together, and how a concept becomes a reality. By showing finished dresses with their designs, patterns, and sketches, we tried to connect all of the dots. I wanted museumgoers to see how a designer moves from an original concept through experimentation and evolution, until the finished product expresses the artist's vision.

The clothing was displayed next to the patterns laid out flat, so that the public could see how these jigsaw pieces of paper would magically morph into sinewy, slinky dresses or deceptively simple cloth cocoons. I have always appreciated ingenuity of cut and economy of line. Now, I was thrilled to help continue the dialogue of design by showing my work to other designers and aficionados in a museum setting.

One of the biggest challenges in preparing the Toledo/Toledo exhibit lay in deciding how to present our work cohesively. At first we considered doing the exhibit along a traditional time line, presenting the earliest garments first and moving through my designs year by year as in a traditional retrospective exhibition.

However, the more we all thought about it, the more we realized that there was another, more informative and interesting way to present the exhibit. Since I am fueled by my interest in how things are constructed, I allowed this idea to be pivotal. Rather than present my work as wearable art in chronological order, we chose to make the dialogue come alive even more vibrantly by presenting the connections among concepts, aesthetics, utility, and engineering.

It became evident that we should group the garments according to their physical qualities, almost like one would group species in a zoo, or how family members are organized in genealogy charts. This would make for a much more educational experience. We could show the garments side by side, regardless of when they were designed.

Of course, there was some design overlap, but we could clearly see that certain garments fell into distinct categories. I had been using names for these categories all along. Now I was excited to use these categories to group the clothes according to the physical presence of my ideas in the garments, and thus define these different themes and design visions to share with the public.

It was especially important for me to share these designs ideas with students. Having mentored fashion design students at several colleges, I had realized that one of the essential missing links in their education was the connection between imagination and results. It often wasn't clear to students and interns what steps would get them from an initial idea, through the work process, and on to a final result. These steps had become a lost art to many students in fashion.

Categorizing my work for the Toledo/Toledo exhibit—which went on from New York to travel to Kent State University Museum in Ohio, the Museum at Otis College of Art and Design in Los Angeles, and to museums and galleries in Vienna, London, Tokyo, and other locations afterward—was enormously educational for both Ruben and me. We could see how we'd evolved both as individual artists and as a collaborative couple.

This collaborative experience also became a focus of the exhibition, since Ruben and I don't just collaborate with each other, but with many friends as well. Since we came of age in the creative stew that was New York City in the late 1970s and early 1980s, Ruben and I understand the value of cross-pollinating ideas. We wanted young fashion students to understand the importance of working with other people who have different points of views and skill sets from their own.

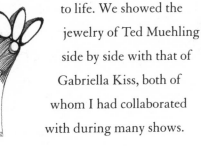

For example, in the exhibit we paid tribute to hair artists Orlando Pita and Danillo, who had designed amazing hair concepts for many of my early shows. Images of the models on the runways to were featured in the exhibitions, bringing the

thrill of these presentations to life. We showed the jewelry of Ted Muehling side by side with that of Gabriella Kiss, both of whom I had collaborated with during many shows.

We also displayed some of the shoe designs I had collaborated on with Manolo Blahnik.

Simon Doonan helped us fine-tune the exhibition, with his eagle eye for creating mise-en-scènes with humor. The book and catalog were designed by our friends, Stephen Gan, James Kaliardos, and Cecilia Dean with their *Visionaire* team. The mannequins, of course, were all designed by Ruben, and showcased his professional collaborations with Ralph Pucci's mannequins.

The experience of working on "Toledo/ Toledo: A Marriage of Art and Fashion" was an illuminating one. Never had I the luxury of time to step back and examine the evolution of my own design process. Now, since I wasn't holding seasonal runway shows, I was able to take the time to analyze the full scope of my designs and do just that. Allowing ourselves to examine how we work together was very telling of what it means to share a language, how it affects one another's output.

THE EVOLUTION OF MY DESIGN PROCESS

By now, I had been designing collections and collaborating for many years with Ruben. Yet, as we put together the FIT exhibit, I realized that there was still no one set method or one concrete design process that I followed. For me, ideas take on a life of their own, and I often go where they lead me.

The only thing these ideas have in common is that they all start in my head, either from the challenge of visualizing an emotion, an encounter with a technical breakthrough, or simply the thrill of ingenuity. I work out design concepts internally first, thinking through a concept from start to finish. Imagining a flat idea and growing it into a three-dimensional form can happen in many ways.

I imagine that in many ways I explore like an architect. I like that concept and feeling of space. The curve of a wall inside a structure and the emotion it provokes might make me think about a curve in a garment. Clothing patterns are like architecture blueprints to me: I can imagine how those flat patterns will look and feel on my body.

Once I have that thought clarified in my own mind, I describe it to Ruben and usually demonstrate it by draping a piece of fabric to mimic what I'm thinking about. Or I might fold a bit of paper or describe an action with my hands. Ruben then draws the shapes in a way that he thinks expresses my concept.

I'll keep playing with a design in my head and experimenting with different versions of the same thought while Ruben documents my ideas and emotions on paper with a thousand variations. This documentation of my ideas serves as a design diary and catalog of concepts for further development. I would estimate that we've brought to life a mere ten percent of the work in the diaries. For me, designing clothes is like playing jazz: You can do a million variations using the same few notes. By now, Ruben and I have a whole library of sketchbooks cataloged by year. I call this our "constant conversation."

In arranging the Toledo/Toledo exhibit with Dr. Steele according to the concepts embedded in my designs, I was better able to understand and talk about the evolution of my ideas. The exhibition's primary categories included Origami, Shape, Suspension, Shadow, Organic Geometry, and Liquid Architecture. Through viewing the exhibit by these concepts, museumgoers could really see how fashion design is similar to architecture or to any other design discipline. It has a solid, concrete foundation, and is about much more than what you see on the surface. Part of the allure of fashion is its decorative outward appearance, but true fashion design is as solid as engineering and built on sound ideas.

Perhaps the most important thing about putting together this show and grouping my garments to demonstrate my thinking was the realization that I, the woman who was once too shy to speak, had developed a design language to communicate my ideas and emotions.

PLAYING WITH ORIGAMI

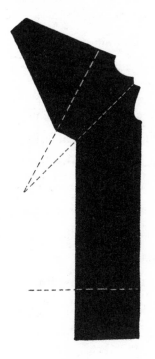

The Japanese developed Origami into a high art form, creating intricate three-dimensional shapes by folding flat pieces of paper in complex ways. From my earliest days of making paper boats to float after rainstorms in my native Camajuani, Cuba, I have been deeply intrigued by the challenge of creating a complex form by using simple geometric shapes that I can drape and fold into three-dimensional sculptures. I have always played with paper; even now, whenever I'm seated at a table, I will fold my napkin or scraps of whatever paper is handy, twisting the paper into abstract shapes to see where my hands and gestures can take me.

One of my earliest experiments with origami led me straight to my tube jacket. This jacket, when laid out flat, looks like calligraphy or a punctuation point. This was part of my elementary phase of sewing and designing clothes. In teaching myself how to make patterns, I folded my way into a denim jacket made from one piece of cloth. This is minimalism in action—the least amount of sewing and cutting as possible. I lined the jacket in the brightest cotton madras for shock appeal and visual warmth. When worn, this construction feels like a friendly pair of arms hugging you constantly from behind. More complex versions of this construction idea continue to bloom each season. One of the best has been a waterproof fire hose linen version that demonstrates how a few pieces of two-dimensional cloth shapes transform into a three-dimensional jacket with arced lapels and a back shaped like a sail.

The zigzag dress is also a simple solution to shaping a dress through folds. The concept was to create a wave from a straight line. The wave is cut out of one piece of cloth. This dress came to me, quite literally, as I was fiddling with a piece of paper. The neckline shape is repeated six times and traced while slightly changing the angles. The winding cascade of repetition flows down to the hemline and eventually wraps around the entire body. The result looks deceptively simple and graceful, hiding its inner mathematical equation.

SHAPE

Shape is what I call my elementary stage. This is where I played with very simple kitelike forms to build a more abstract concept of the human body. Directing geometric shapes to correspond to the human form became my design language.

I have always been enamored by shapes. From the early days of my childhood, when I used to play with the simple nuts and bolts in the storeroom of my father's hardware store, I have been drawn to try to put together different shapes and different materials. The world is one giant puzzle with many smaller puzzles making up the whole.

It is the same reason that I dissected paintings of the Masters in school by painting just a tiny segment at a time: I wanted to isolate the lyrical line that spoke to me best or find the basic shapes that went into making something more complex that was so intricate and pleasing to the eye.

My work, in some ways, reflects an "East Meets West" approach to design, in the sense that I was taking flat patterns (East) and tailoring just part of them (West). For instance, instead of making flat rectangular pattern shapes, like what you might use to construct a kimono, I was using circles to make more flowing romantic lines to achieve an abstract volume, still packable. I used this concept to make handbags and carryalls. These eventually morphed into entire garments. A lot of my earliest designs featured curved hemlines; I saw those hems as gestures, and called them my "speed lines." I wanted to capture a sense of action and motion. A straight hem seemed to be still and frozen in time. A harmonious and continuous curve from the upper thigh dipping back to cover the back of the knees freed up the stride and looked as if you were walking even when standing still. I had created them after watching Ruben draw and thinking about his rapid, fluid arm motions as he does calligraphy.

SUSPENSION: A LOVE OF ENGINEERING AND ARCHITECTURE

The idea of "suspension" for a garment came from my love of engineering, which I first developed as a child, marveling at the way my grandmother's sewing machine was engineered. I also remember how awestruck I was when my family first crossed the Pulaski Skyway, that steel cantilever bridge connecting Newark and Jersey City. The ingenious methods of suspending something so massive as a bridge with such grace and precision continue to inspire me.

"Suspension" is the term I use to describe my dress designs that are stripped down to their central architecture. By suspending the entire dress design from one central core, a garment can harmoniously flow while keeping its balance and collapse while still maintaining a pleasing shape.

The Suspender dress from 1997 is the most obvious example of this. The skirt front and back is woven in and out of the simple T-shirt-like torso and rests on one shoulder safely holding up the entire dress. The shifting of the waistline, up or down, creates a different waist size.

Another dress that demonstrates this concept is the Caterpillar dress, which I first made in 1998. I cut this dress with one long continuous curved seam that winds around the front and back of the body. The dress on a hanger has its weight all on the one seam. The pattern of this dress when seen flat resembles two fish swimming in opposite directions fused together.

SHADOW: THE INTERPLAY OF TRANSPARENT AND OPAQUE

I've always been attracted by the way that light and shadow create different designs and different moods. With fabric, I am constantly experimenting with how transparent fabrics can be combined to achieve depth. The word "shadow" is something I started using to describe my way of creating mystery by playing with cloth.

Even as a teenager, I experimented with the concept of creating shadow by making abstract modern tops and skirts out of old doilies and antique lace curtains from flea markets. Perhaps I come by this love of lace genetically, since my mother's aunts all made their own, but I am constantly intrigued by the mysterious, provocative way that using lace on bare skin or against other fabrics seems like calligraphy or the ancient art of tribal tattooing. Before I could sew, I was pulling threads out of textiles to loosen the weave. This was my attempt at creating my own naïve version of lace—through deconstruction. I love the empty space in the weave of a fabric; this allows a textile to breathe and facilitates a graceful silhouette. Gravity plays a crucial role in open-weave fabrics.

The concept of shadow and lace does not have to necessarily be revealing. In fact, one of my favorite wedding dresses I ever made for a client was practically weatherproof. The bride-to-be was getting married in an unheated country barn. I embroidered cotton wadding with thick waxed thread in

an abstract, calligraphy-like scroll, creating the illusion of
a story written on the dress itself. This covered the entire
geometrically cut skirt and bomber jacket. This was all
protected by sheer cotton organdy. The heavy quilting seemed
as light as a delicate floating puffy cloud. Perfect for my
Japanese client who was a meteorologist.

ORGANIC GEOMETRY

"Organic geometry" is something I love
to do: transform the logical and
simple into the mysterious. One
of my earliest designs to fall
into this category and to be
featured in the first Toledo/
Toledo exhibition was the
beach ball bag I made and
sold at Fiorucci in 1984 out
of orange, yellow, and pink
burlap. This design soon morphed
into the Packing Dress, which
purely embodies the concept of organic
geometry. This dress facilitates the practical need to fold, or in

this case, roll an article of clothing down to the smallest possible size for a suitcase or a bureau drawer. When it is unrolled, the dress reveals its voluminous and luxurious proportions, made from two simple circles sewn together—one white, the other black. I crafted the neckline and armhole openings on one black circle. The hem opening is created out of one perfectly cut circle floating off center inside the white circle. When the two circles are sewn together, the different openings don't overlap; this means that, when the wearer dons the dress, the flat circles are able to transform from pure geometric flat forms into a wearable and graceful geodesic dome.

The transformation of geometric pattern shapes into amorphic forms is what I like to call "romantic mathematics"—the simple logic of math made mysteriously amorphic with the help of gravity.

My jelly fish blouses are the most versatile use of this concept. Made from only one-pattern pieces, the same pattern shape can be folded in various ways to create four different silhouettes, from a bubblelike top to a flowing winged tunic. This versatility demonstrates pure American innovation to me.

THE EVOLUTION OF LIQUID ARCHITECTURE

Liquid architecture is how we came to describe the structured lines and seams that hold in shape my jersey designs. I love working in jersey because of its pull and give. Its fluidity can be shaped with strategic seaming.

It took me many years of experimenting on myself to design and develop jersey dresses that would have more shape and structure than the jersey dresses I saw in stores that so often hung like tubes on a woman's body.

After years of experimenting with draping and seaming on different machines, I developed methods of shaping jersey using thick, welted seams made on a sewing machine used to sew undergarments. My jersey dresses seem to drip off the wearer's body yet retain a structure that sometimes appears to challenge gravity. I deliberately "build" these dresses so that they cut away from a woman's body rather than cling to her.

By 1993, I had developed my Kangaroo dress. The dress starts off suspended from the shoulder blades and then drapes around the front torso to form a deep, gracefully cowled pocket, which gives the dress its name.

AFTER TOLEDO/TOLEDO: MANIPULATED SURFACES AND OTHER REVELATIONS

Putting together the Toledo/Toledo show taught me a great deal about my own process and designs. It also served as a turning point in my career. After taking stock of my design vocabulary, I was able to see how all of those ideas and concepts  had evolved into new hybrids. Like a DNA chain, my designs endlessly unfurled into new variations. Now I was ready to expand my design vocabulary by doing something completely different.

I have never designed something just for the sake of decoration. To me, that would be like cheating. I enjoy decoration and ornamentation as much as the next person, but I like to invest my time in design ideas that are more permanent. After the Toledo/Toledo show, I went even further into manipulating textiles and morphing them into new textures and surfaces with unique properties. I started incorporating the fabric itself to form new design elements as a way of meeting the challenge of using even more sophisticated couture techniques in my work. I sought to push the boundaries of what I could do as a seamstress in my next attempts to express myself in novel ways through fabric and fashion design.

The phrase "manipulated surfaces" refers to how I enhance a garment's structure by playing with the ground fabric I use to make an article of clothing. For example, I use a patchwork method for ruching lightweight jersey, sewing together smaller pieces of cloth that I first flute or pleat. The overall effect is a lightweight dress that is still flattering, despite the different layers quilted together, because I make sure that the gathered panels don't add bulk to the dress.

I also use this phrase to describe how I create my own multidimensional fabrics, like my Rattan Armor jackets and Waterfall dresses, which I sculpt from textiles that are so densely pleated, they're almost rigid, despite being made out of soft, fluid cloths. One design with especially deep pleats is my Armadillo Sleeve shirtwaist dress, which really does resemble armor, as well as my Fringed Shoulder gown, a dress that I made in black silk tulle, then embroidered with multicolored silk floss.

Ruben helps me manipulate surfaces as well. I created a design that I call my Broomstick Librarian dress. This dress has a traditional shirtwaist silhouette, but we played with the fabric for our Anne Klein Spring/Summer 2008 collection by soaking undyed silk pongee in water and tightly twisting it around a pole. We let the fabric dry before unwinding it from the pole, in a technique that was originally developed by Native American women in our own Southwest.

Overall, the Toledo/Toledo exhibition explored the themes that thread their way throughout my entire body of work over the past twenty-seven years. Organic geometry transforms geometric patterns into amorphous shapes. Shadow explores the interplay of the transparent and the opaque. Liquid architecture is used to describe my method of building in shape, using seams to give structure to the most pliable of textiles. Other themes include suspension—the exploration of balancing the core structure of a dress or garment with the use of one central point, like the backbone of your body, or the trunk of a tree. Shape is how I refer to my elementary stage, the main geometric shapes that form the base of the body of my work. These shapes can be morphed, transformed and combined endlessly to create new variations. Origami refers to garments formed by the folding of patterns. The silhouette of a dress is formed by the repetition of the patterns. These garments offer a comprehensive view of the interrelationships of all the concepts that I developed and the creative output of both Ruben and me.

LANDING ON OUR FEET

Since I was no longer on the endless treadmill of always preparing for the next fashion show, I was now free to invest all of my time and resources into my technical explorations and creative work. There was a new creative blooming at the House of Toledo. The FIT exhibition exposed me to a much wider audience, as students and the museumgoing public became more aware of my design language. Some new and interesting collaborations soon blossomed as a result.

One of the most challenging was with the great American choreographer Twyla Tharp. Twyla is one of America's most original thinkers, as gutsy and individualistic as her work. Her dance pieces are full of the magic of mathematical precision and mysterious inner rhythms. She had seen our first exhibit at FIT, Toledo/Toledo, and contacted me to ask if I would collaborate on a project with her.

We had never met before, but Twyla had fallen in love with the Hermaphrodite dress the moment she saw it at the FIT exhibit. She now wanted to use it, along with other designs she had spotted in the exhibition, for a new piece she was choreographing for the American Ballet Theatre. The Hermaphrodite dress was, and still is, one of my favorite prototypes, so I excitedly agreed to work with her.

This collaboration was a technical challenge because of the nature of dance performances; the action and movement involved was the easy part, because my clothes are made for action, but the frequency with which the clothing has to be worn becomes an issue. The constant wear and tear of performance clothing is way beyond what the normal usage of my designs would be.

Twyla's new dance piece was called *Yemaya*, and it was
an abstract homage to the Cuban cabaret
atmosphere of the 1950s and to the
Santeria religion, set to the
music of the Cuban group
the Buena Vista
Social Club. We
dressed most of
the female dancers
in variations of my Pulley dress.
When the wearer is standing still,
this dress hangs perfectly slim, like an
elegant, column-shaped garment. When the
dancers moved, they had all of the freedom they
needed, because of the way the dress is cut. The
deceptive pyramid-like construction is held up
by an integrated scarf that winds up the front of
the dress and loops back down. This dress was
born for movement. On their toes, the dancers moved like
cabaret dancers in high heels, a glamorous and innovative
choreography choice.

For the male dancers in the production, I soft-tailored
sharp white suits with neat, narrow pant legs, designing them
with enough gussets to accommodate the rigorous leaps and

turns. The jackets were cut like the ones I have been making for Ruben since 1985, with my signature gusset sleeves to accommodate high reaching movements.

The uniformity of the male dancers in white linen suits presented a graphic formal setting and background for the poetic and mysterious geometric movements. The whole Twyla Tharp Dance Troupe merged and morphed into a cohesive whole, undulating like a dangerous, sensuous reptile dressed in an Isabel Toledo skin.

The lead female dancer wore the Hermaphrodite dress in chiffon. She was carried like a goddess, tossed about like a flower, and turned upside down during this performance.

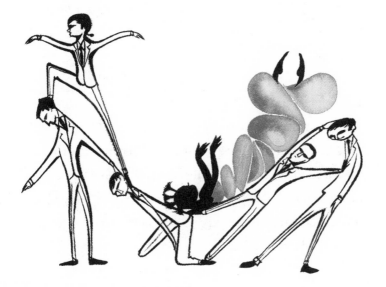

Twyla invited us to see the work in progress during rehearsals several times throughout its development. I knew it would be a stunning piece, and I could already imagine the dancers costumed. Nonetheless, I was not prepared for the overwhelming beauty of the final effect.

I had the privilege of attending a performance of *Yemaya* in upstate New York. I don't know how Twyla could have predicted how the rings on the Hermaphrodite dress would billow out and fill with air as the dancer jumped, becoming a hard form, and then deflate again, emphasizing her movements. For my part, I was astonished. This was truly poetry in motion. Once again, I realized that the most successful collaborations are those where the total result achieves the magic of alchemy.

REAPING WHAT I SEW

My studio and I continued to rise to new heights as I eagerly continued to explore more challenging techniques. I like to remind young fashion students that it takes years and years to perfect your craft. To master anything in life, you have to give it time, dedication, and focus.

My earliest designs were composed of elementary shapes reduced to their purest form. Now, my work took on a very tactile, controlled aesthetic. My shapes all bloomed into what I called "manipulated surfaces." Believe me, this was no small achievement. We had always been self-propelled, with no visible means of support or backing of any kind, and this new type of work took a great deal of fabric and many hours of labor to achieve.

Fortunately, I was blessed with consistent accounts, like Barneys, Nordstrom, Ikram in Chicago, Colette in Paris, Septième Étage in Geneva, and Joyce in Hong Kong. I also had a loyal clientele mostly made up of professional women who appreciate the art of clothes. They understand the difference between fashion created and manufactured in the corporate environment of a brand, and the intimate tradition of couture, meaning a dress made by an artist.

In the best scenarios, well-crafted, mass-produced brands and exquisitely executed couture concepts coexist harmoniously. One without the other leads to sameness and extinction. In the growing fashion expansion, we designers also get to explore the challenge of designing for the mass market. This is a discipline that takes equal parts concept, make, manufacturing, and—perhaps most importantly—the bottom line of price.

Mixing many different levels of quality and labels in our wardrobes is what makes each of us so individual, because we can mix and match our looks to suit our lifestyles. This makes my job a pleasure. It is yet another collaboration to see your work interpreted by others as part of fashion's continuous dialogue. I believe in this high and low idea. This is how I suspect most of us grew up. It has always been part of the American fashion identity.

THE COOPER-HEWITT AWARD: "I AM THE HAPPIEST WOMAN IN THE WORLD."

When our studio was selected as the winner of the Smithsonian Museum's Cooper-Hewitt National Design Award for Fashion in 2005, it was pure joy and surprise. For me, this was total validation that fashion design can transcend taste and trends and be appreciated as a formal design discipline.

Fashion's unique position in design is complex. The elements of taste and decoration, style and flair all come into play, not to mention the psychological components involved in dressing. Clothing being such an intimate and personal human appendage, it is easy to lose sight of its fundamental core.

I had been featured in the Cooper-Hewitt Design Triennial Exhibition just one year prior to winning the award. Our exhibition consisted of some of my designs laid out flat on the wall like giant jigsaw puzzles, next to the same designs displayed on Ruben's mannequins. This allowed the viewer to see the metamorphosis my clothes underwent in the wearing.

I was very pleased at that time to be called a "radical classicist" by curator Susan Yelavich. As much as I don't like being labeled, this description seems to fit me well. I love what is classic and can stand the test of time. I love longevity and ideas that can be built upon, layer by layer. On the other hand, I believe in thinking for yourself. When designers think for themselves, they arrive at ideas that are purely theirs. And, when something is new, it is radical by nature—not for the sake of rebellion, but because it is unfamiliar.

This complex "radical classicist" quality that Susan Yelavich perceived in my work can be found in most of my clothes from the very start. As much as I love the classics, I feel the need to go beyond that with my work. I like to think that I am designing future classics.

Why did winning the Cooper-Hewitt Award mean so much, when Ruben and I had already been established for so many years and were doing what we loved to do? I think it was because it represented an appreciation for the individual design voice. As we had experienced firsthand, it's all too easy to get squeezed out of the fashion scene by the big fashion machinery when you're a small, independent design studio. I was thrilled because this award was the biggest recognition possible in fashion design, and it was based not on personality, social connections, or our business model, but solely on the unique qualities that Ruben and I expressed in the body of our work. This recognition was a vote for individuality and independence in fashion design, and evidence that the strength

of our design work and vision over the last twenty years had
been absorbed by the culture at large.

The Cooper-Hewitt awards are held yearly to celebrate
American design in the fields of architecture, graphic design,
and industrial design. The ceremony is held at the Cooper-
Hewitt National Museum of Design, a New York branch of the
Smithsonian. To receive the award was a double gift, because we
were presented this honor by our good friend, Simon Doonan of
Barneys. To be recognized for your achievement and have that
award be presented to you by someone who is a member of your
creative family is the height of accomplishment.

Ruben and I were in a daze from all of the excitement on
the night of the awards dinner. We had never won anything
and were trying not to be too optimistic. But Ruben jumped
to his feet as soon as Simon announced that he'd first met this
year's winners in the fashion category at the Metropolitan
Museum's Costume Institute twenty years earlier. I just sat
there for a minute and cried—tears of happiness.

I really was the happiest woman in the world at that
moment. To share this joy with all of the talent in that room
that night completed my happiness. The only emotion I have
felt that comes close to that is the feeling I had as I watched
Michelle Obama walk down Pennsylvania Avenue wearing
one of my designs on Inauguration Day 2009.

Winning this award took us to the White House for a formal ceremony. This was a big deal for Ruben and me. We had come to this country with our families as political refugees. We had grown up in this land where the promise of freedom and equality are a given. Entering the doors of the White House, we were reminded of the great privilege it is to be living and working in the United States, a self-made country where everyone can pursue their dreams and contribute their spark of originality to the quilt of this American life.

We were blessed to have successfully navigated our way through the rough hustle and bustle of this wide-open cultural territory. Ruben and I had defined our personal vision through our work, and had the privilege of helping to define our time. And, as if this weren't exciting enough, we were actually being invited into the White House to be honored by Laura Bush, along with the other award winners!

Walking through the corridors of the White House, we were extremely conscious of the fact that we were stepping on the floors where many presidents had walked before us. The structure of the White House is elegant, yet it seems as low-key, solid, and reliable as most Americans are. Every square inch of it is permeated with a rich, complex history that you can feel as you enter the building. Ruben and I were in awe of the libraries that seemed to be tucked into every nook and corner.

Even the women's lounge is a real treat. I had to break the women-only rule and sneak Ruben into it, so that he could see the portrait of Eleanor Roosevelt hanging there. She is a personal all-time favorite of mine, because she helped to champion so many women's causes. She was also one of the original founders of Fashion Group International (FGI), an organization that helped promote design awareness in the U.S. as a way of helping garment workers, who were mostly women and immigrants. A year later, I felt that Eleanor herself had blessed Ruben and me, when we received a Fashion Visionary Award from FGI.

The luncheon itself went by in a haze of excitement. Laura Bush addressed the roomful of journalists and congratulated us all on this honor. What struck me was how wonderful it is that this award, first conceived in 1997 and launched in 2000 as part of the White House Millennium Council, specifically honored lasting achievements in American design that recognize excellence, innovation, and enhancement of the quality of life. The awards keep innovation in the creative fields a possibility for all; winning one has nothing to do with what school you attended or what grades you achieve to earn this honor. The awards are based purely on contributions to culture.

During the ceremony, we were all especially mesmerized by Eva Zeisel, an extraordinary designer also being honored with a Lifetime Achievement Award. A native of Budapest, Eva worked in the modern ceramic industry and was eventually named Artistic Director for the Porcelain and Glass Industries of Russia. She has designed more than 100,000 objects centered on the home and table. Eva is a fascinating talent, full of creative energy that flows gracefully from her hands.

In fact, Eva spoke mostly with her hands when she accepted her award, and that was fine, because no words were necessary. Her rare and talented hands were capable of molding her sentiments out of thin air. Her work in ceramic and glass is like an echo of her personality, and is formed with the same gentle wit and humanity.

It was an honor for us to be recognized at the same time as this legendary artist, whose work in ceramics has made history many times over. Eva, and artists like her, are high up on my totem pole of inspiration. To achieve success on your own personal terms, and to be gifted with the ability to share your life's experience with others through your work for a lifetime, are rare treasures to cherish.

ANNE KLEIN CALLING

"Anne Klein is on the line," Ruben shouted to me one day. He had a paintbrush in one hand as he gave me the phone with the other.

When the Jones New York people called me to discuss a collaboration with Anne Klein, I nearly fell off my chair.

Anne Klein was one of my fashion heroes. She started a career in fashion as a sketcher when she was only a teenager. She really did grow up in the American fashion industry, and she knew it like the back of her hand. It was truly the Garment District then, and not yet the rarefied world of designers it was to become. The Garment District was where most of America got dressed, with wardrobes being made right here in New York City's midtown.

Tragically, Anne Klein died of breast cancer in 1974 at age fifty, but in the few short years that she and her husband, Matthew Rubinstein, owned and operated the Anne Klein Design House, she had changed the American fashion vocabulary. Her business vision and understanding of the modern woman's life transformed retail, first here in the U.S., and later across the world. It's easy to take her trailblazing vision for granted now, but Anne Klein really provided women with the key to move forward in fashion. Her development of a modular, gridlike system of dressing with pieces that could be mixed, matched, and recombined in endless possibilities was revolutionary in its day. Her way of thinking is very much an instinctive part of my design DNA.

Now, in 2006, I was being offered the opportunity to be the creative director of Anne Klein, who along with Claine McCardle and Bonnie Cashin, is one of the original founding mothers of true blue American sportswear. This was both a real privilege and a huge undertaking. I was coming from running a hands-on business, where everything really is handmade. If I accepted this position, I would be working with one of the largest manufacturers in the U.S.

The CEO, Peter Boneparth, explained, that he wanted to strengthen the core of the brand by introducing a designer division. The name Anne Klein had grown to include many diffusion lines because of its popularity and appeal among women. He understood that, in the overcrowded landscape of fashion retail, a brand needs a true core to retain fashion credibility among women.

I was thrilled by the offer. I welcomed this chance to put my design philosophy to work on a larger international scale. I also fully embraced this creative opportunity to further develop clothing design and a system of dressing that is still relevant today, because it is an intelligent solution to that perennial question of what to wear on a daily basis. This can be one of the hardest questions to answer for most women; it is far easier sometimes to find an exquisite dress for a special occasion than it is to figure out your daily look.

When rumors got around that Anne Klein might be considering me as their next creative director, some in the fashion industry questioned this choice. I had acquired the dubious reputation of being a "designer's designer." As seasoned fashion veterans explained to me, this distinction could be interpreted as the kiss of death in a Mafia movie instead of a compliment.

It can be hard for some to see beyond packaging or style to the engineered bones of a design. Since I had become well known for making couture-quality clothes, many wondered whether I had the ability to design more casual day clothes. They couldn't see that a good structure is a good structure, whether you're making garments for an individual woman or for a mass market. What counts is the architecture of a design. They had also apparently forgotten that most of my early collections were made of denim, and were mostly casual day clothes.

DURING MY BRIEF ASSOCIATION WITH Anne Klein, I was able to indulge in my love for uniform dressing, cultivating a very clean and extreme silhouette that was both true to Anne's way of thinking and a step forward into the future. What I designed for Anne Klein were actually clothes that I would have been doing for my own collection, if I'd had the facilities to produce and distribute on a large scale.

Making a ready-to-wear collection on a mass scale involves producing many pieces in bulk so that the prices can come down to an affordable level. It's a general rule that, the greater the quantity you're producing of a particular style, the more you can negotiate the price of textiles and bring down the cost of manufacturing. There is a challenge embedded in this general rule, though: All separate items have to be shipped at the right time in order to get complete looks into the store and allow women to play the important role of fashion director and stylist for themselves.

This is where the magic begins, with consumers participating in American sportswear and women deciding how they will put their wardrobes together. My job as a designer for Anne Klein was to supply the raw material so that women could make it into fashion. Handing fashion power over to consumers is the direct opposite of working in an ivory tower. Women can be tempted by the suggestions and innovations from designers, but they can't be dictated to; the female consumer is therefore in the driver's seat. Fashion must go where she decides, because she votes with her wallet.

This kind of independent thinking fuels me, and getting to design under the Anne Klein label seemed like the stars had aligned. Anne Klein and I were working in different times and with different circumstances, but she and I were both very much believers in not talking down to women. We both believed that intelligent clothes earn a place of honor in your wardrobe, because these are the items you reach for again and again. These are the old friends that keep surprising you with their versatility.

There were several hurdles to conquer right at the start of my tenure as creative director. First, there was the Fashion Week deadline. Did we want to show an Anne Klein collection this first season, or skip a season and then premiere? It was late in the season, and I would really have to boogie to get it together in time. There was a design room team to pull together, a showroom to build, and a collection to design, sew, and merchandise in just three months if I wanted to show a collection for the 2007 Fall/Winter season.

WE TACKLED THE SHOWROOM FIRST, since it would take heavy construction. I needed to get this part going to be ready to greet new buyers after the show. The home base for Jones is right in the hub of the Garment District, at the top of a building at

38th and Seventh Avenue. The space was high up in the building, with an exceptional view of midtown Manhattan. I wanted to make the most of this powerful vision, because this view represented Anne Klein as a powerful New York woman.

We designed a minimal glass room, transparent and light, with the heaviest, most Baroque doorframes in a delicate pink marble. The doorframes served as a gentle feminine counterpoint to the backdrop of soot-covered steel gray buildings just outside the windows. The collection would have a happy home nesting up in the clouds, surrounded by the Manhattan skyline. I could feel the energy and vibrancy of the city in this view. I wanted to capture that in the clothes and, through the clothes, give back some of the city's energy to the women who wore my Anne Klein designs.

We veiled the transparent showroom in nude industrial mesh curtains when privacy was required, which made the space feel modern and playful. We also designed a connected meeting room. This was like a clubhouse, with a cozy nook upholstered in white leather that we nicknamed "The Think Tank," because it would serve as a place where we could refuel and rest, or hold one-on-one strategy meetings.

The whole showroom was constructed with harmony and vibrancy in mind. The result was that nobody ever wanted to leave it. Whenever I design an environment for living or working, this is exactly what I try to achieve. Since Ruben and I have always lived and worked in our work space, I know how important it is to have the environment you spend most of your day in be full of energy and efficiency to make work a pleasure—especially when creating things of beauty.

Designing the collection for Anne Klein took a lot of focus and determination. My concept was refined and streamlined. Staying true to Anne Klein's vision, I made the wardrobe the main ingredient and primary focus. I wanted women to be able to layer onto it, adding to its core without replacing it. This is how a woman begins to define herself and forge an identity. The whole point of the collection was to free women from having to think too much about their clothes. They could look great but be free to live their lives.

"Couture-haberdashery" became the nickname that stuck for this first Anne Klein collection. I never name a collection at the start, but while my staff and I are working, certain names and descriptions seem to stick. This one defined that first collection best. I wanted to give women the ease and uncomplicated correctness of a man's wardrobe, made with the secrets and surprising elements of couture. The clothes possessed an inner charm and mystery, while being basic enough for a woman to reach for on a daily basis. These were clothes destined to find their way into a woman's daily menu of "must wear," not "must have." My wardrobe closet today is rich with the pieces I made for Anne Klein, and to this day, I am approached by women that hold on to the pieces they bought from my time at AK.

I was thrilled to have the opportunity to make clothes for the no-nonsense woman. We have enough complications in life, and clothes should simplify our lives. Designing shoes and handbags to complete the look was also a real luxury, especially because I had the opportunity at Anne Klein to collaborate with Italian leather makers and take a tour of Old World craftsmanship.

I WAS PLEASED WITH MY first Anne Klein designs, and very proud that Ruben and I had pulled it off. For Fashion Week, I purposefully avoided falling into the trap of staging an ultra-slick production; instead I tried to capture the simplicity and aura of individuality. I wanted to let the clothes speak for themselves, because the imperfection of real life is always more interesting and satisfying to me than fantasy.

My Anne Klein collection received the only standing ovation of that season's Fashion Week, and most of the reviews were favorable enough to earn a good response from retailers.

Now the trick would be to produce and ship all of the items at the highest possible standard.

I had already become well known for the high quality make of my own collection, so the bar was raised as high as you can get. I was delighted when a whole team arrived in New York City from China to work with me directly in producing the collection for retail. To make sure that all of the details were well explained and understood, it was necessary to work face-to-face.

The level of effort that the Chinese team invested into producing the collection was impressive. Some of the tailors had learned their craft in Hong Kong many years ago. Hong Kong had been a hub of tailoring and manufacturing since the 1960s, so I sensed that we were in good hands. Still, when the production arrived and was ready to ship out to stores, I tried on many of the garments myself. I wanted to feel the fit and make sure that we could all be proud when the clothes hit the selling floor.

What I loved most about this first experience designing for a powerhouse like Anne Klein was meeting the women customers who wore Anne Klein clothes. From New York to San Francisco, and almost any city in between, women came out of the woodwork to talk about their personal experiences with Anne Klein clothing. One woman confessed, "I bought my first dress for work from Anne Klein in 1972!" Another told me that those were the very first fashion items she had ever bought with her own money, and that she still owned them.

Everyone's love for Anne Klein came up, whether we were talking with younger customers or their mothers. This kind of emotional attachment is hard to come by in fashion. I felt a personal responsibility toward these women to continue offering them as many innovative solutions to dressing as I could muster, season after season. I sensed that women had been waiting for fashion that empowered them.

The Anne Klein designer collection that I produced was meant to represent every kind of woman; it was inclusive in its design scope. This was a tall order, because we are a big country with many different climates and lifestyles. This much diversity is one of our strengths. My Anne Klein collection would allow a woman to mix and match, or even mismatch, her clothes in ways that would represent her individual style and ever-changing emotions. As a designer, I like to think that I am clothing a woman's mind and mood as well as her body. Creating clothes that spoke to so many different kinds of women, in their various life roles and moods, had always been one of my key goals as a designer. Now I had done it on a large scale.

. . .

ALL IN ALL, I WAS able to design three full collections for Anne Klein's designer division. Resort we had called "industrial glamour" for the clean and polished fabrics cut with razorlike precision, before the company pulled the plug. Spring became "art attack," mostly for the raw and unexpected use of color and the accidental brushstrokes that became my iconic hand-painted shirtdresses. The top management changed halfway through my tenure there, and the new powers-that-be decided that they would change their strategy going forward and no longer produce a designer collection.

This was sad news for me, because I really believed that we had set a new standard for what mass American fashion can be. We had achieved a style that extended the versatility of American sportswear, while offering innovative cuts and silhouettes to the American woman. I designed pieces that didn't recapitulate what was already in her wardrobe, but instead complemented what she already owned. By adding and subtracting, layering and moving pieces around, a woman could create an endless number of looks. These kinds of clothes made pure fashion seem old-fashioned.

COUTURE FOR SURE

This exercise in designing for such a giant powerhouse of American fashion was a revelation to me. I had experienced how the giant fashion machinery works, and how every part of that machinery must function together as smoothly as possible. In my own small business, invention, production, delivery, and sales had to be carried out in a harmonious rhythm; the same was true of Anne Klein, only on a huge scale.

One major difference between a small and large business, of course, is that in a small business, the reaction time is much quicker. We can afford to follow our instincts and make a quick turnabout according to a hunch. It is a much smaller and lighter ship that we're piloting. But, in the end, we are both in the service of women.

Mine is to design clothes as individual and varied as the women who will wear them. Some designs become a main fashion staple for many, while others are a one-off design, like a missing link in my chain of design species. These design missing links are essential for the evolution of a designer. This freedom to experiment is the spark of creativity. This is what links fashion to art. Couture is the very definition of this. A dress made by an artist is the purest definition of couture.

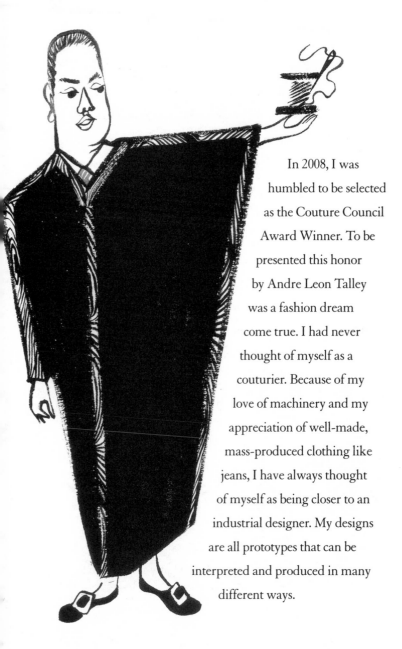

In 2008, I was
humbled to be selected
as the Couture Council
Award Winner. To be
presented this honor
by Andre Leon Talley
was a fashion dream
come true. I had never
thought of myself as a
couturier. Because of my
love of machinery and my
appreciation of well-made,
mass-produced clothing like
jeans, I have always thought
of myself as being closer to an
industrial designer. My designs
are all prototypes that can be
interpreted and produced in many
different ways.

By contrast, I used to think of couture as something made for just one woman to her specific measurements. Now I understand that the concept of couture is much more than that: It is the freedom an artist has in creation—the freedom to make an uncalculated decision and invent what no one knows she needs yet. It is this power of persuasion that transforms fashion into an art form. Preserving this freedom is vital, because it is here where fashion starts.

When Valerie Steele approached me with the good news about the award, I was thrilled. What's more, FIT was going to be mounting "Isabel Toledo: Fashion from the Inside Out," a major retrospective exhibition of my work in its large gallery museum space. There would be an accompanying book by the same name. It was amazing to think that, just ten years after my first exhibit, "Toledo/Toledo," I was now being given the opportunity to continue my design dialogue with the public.

FASHION FROM THE INSIDE OUT

The title of the new exhibition said it all: My approach has always been very, "What you see is what you get." To know something from the inside out means knowing it like the back of your hand. I am very inspired by how things are constructed, and the insides of my designs ultimately inform how the outside looks.

I had first fallen in love with fashion while interning at the Met's Costume Institute. It was there that I had the opportunity to be exposed to the insides of couture masterpieces. That experience really propelled me to pursue fashion design, because I knew that I had something to add to this design dialogue.

I took the honor of this couture award and the FIT exhibition very seriously. The educational aspect of fashion is a priority for me, because I know firsthand how much of a world this experience can open up for someone. My love of fashion design as a serious discipline, along with the opportunity to hold a large, comprehensive retrospective exhibition spanning my twenty-five-year body of design work, now meant that I would be able to share all of this with a new crop of design students.

The fact that FIT has such an important museum directly connected to its school was another plus. Since FIT is the only museum in the U.S. exclusively devoted to the study of fashion and makes its collections available for serious study and research, it is a golden resource. The museum and its collections are also visited by many other international fashion schools, thus furthering fashion education around the world.

We held marathon photo sessions at our studio with the curator, Patricia Mears, and her husband, photographer William Palmer, to get images ready for the book, typically working past midnight. We photographed most of my designs laid out flat on the ground, so that we could show the actual design lines and visually reveal the engineering concepts in the garments. Others were photographed on Ruben's mannequins and showed the garments from the front, side, and back—as close to a panoramic experience of the clothing as we could capture in two-dimensional images.

Our friend, photographer Ruven Afanador, agreed to collaborate with us to create a portfolio of images, cataloging some of my latest designs and dresses, as I had no visual record of them up to that point. For this portfolio, we had the amazing luck to work with Carmen Dell'Orefice, the legendary woman who started working as a model at the age of thirteen. Carmen had to get permission from her mom back then in order to work with Irving Penn; seeing her in action now, you can understand why people say that true beauty defies time. Ruven and Carmen directed and communicated with each other in ways that only true artists can, in the secret language of silence and glances. Words would destroy this inner communication.

This Ruven Afanador tour of Toledo World was rounded out by Alek Wek, who for me revitalized textures and colors in textiles due to her own remarkable skin tone. Alek's grace, proportions and her striking appearance have had one of the biggest impacts on fashion and its representation in the last ten years. The modeling dynamo Crystal Renn, who has a mind as alert and fine-tuned as her body language, completed this unreal fashion composition. Ruven photographed nonstop for an entire weekend in our freezing-cold studio. The skylight was covered in snow, giving the scene a touch of magic.

WALKING INTO HISTORY

As Ruben recalls, on that chilly January morning when we watched First Lady Michelle Obama wearing my coat and dress while going down Pennsylvania Avenue, we felt like we were levitating around the television with our seamstresses. He is probably right. It was like an out-of-body experience, where you watch what's happening in your life but still can't quite believe that's you.

At the same time, I had been secretly confident that this was the outfit Michelle would choose to wear. The dress and coat I had created had everything this great moment required: hope, joy, optimism, and confidence, just like Michelle, her husband, and most of the nation felt at that moment in history. I had invested all of my best feelings into my work, and I hoped that these feelings would be projected out into the world.

The story of how this infamous coat and dress came into existence is replete with layers, just like the garments themselves. Mrs. Obama had been wearing my clothing years before she became First Lady. I knew this because Mrs. Obama had shopped at Ikram, the superchic Chicago women's clothing store that carried my collection.

I had known Ikram herself since she was just a kid and one of the best sales assistants working for Joan Weinstein in Chicago. Joan's shop, Ultimo, was hailed throughout the country for carrying the very best designer collections since opening its doors in 1969. Joan merged a fashion vision with a sure eye for retail; this is a rare gift that gives a good name to being commercial in the best sense of the word.

I have never considered being commercial a bad idea, if being commercial means being market-minded. Since I have been spoiled by working with really talented retailers since starting in business, the idea of knowing your market and surprising your buyers with innovation seems like a win-win situation for all involved. My customers get to discover and experience new designs, the retailer gets to reap the rewards of a good sell-through on their investment, and I get to innovate further. This kind of fashion interest is what I call "fashion receptivity," and Ikram inherited this kind of fashion talent.

All across the country, the fashion landscape of America is the beneficiary of finely run specialty shops like Ikram. These shops are so in tune with their customers that they can move fashion forward more quickly than an ad campaign. They are truly in the trenches of their customers' fashion lives. Luckily for me, Ikram had connected with my design language and understood my language very early on. And, in Ikram, Mrs. Obama had connected with my design language and understood my work.

THE MAGIC OF LEMONGRASS

Quite honestly, it all started with the fabric. The textile itself began to weave the magic that followed. I have always allowed textiles to lead the way to a new vision, and this time was no different—except that the results were staggering. This was a felted wool lace and reminded me of floating islands connected by one strong and sturdy common thread. The empty spaces gave me the ability to play with the illusion of light escaping from beneath.

I love lace in any form because for me, it is one of the most modern as well as ancient of textiles. This wool lace was an exceptional weave, fragile to the eye, but strong and sturdy. This quality is rare to find and is perfect for molding and tailoring. Warmth was a specific concern for me and my staff. We did not want Michelle to freeze. I wanted this coat and dress to protect the First Lady, to comfort and hug her like a friend, while still allowing her relaxed body language to shine through and speak.

I backed the lace in thin layers of cream silk radzimir and cloudlike silk netting. Sandwiching the interlinings were thin weblike stitches of pashmina for extra warmth. The cream silk lining showing through the eyelet of the lace created the illusion of sunlight hitting water. This glittering light effect had many experienced fashion folks declaring the dress was made of sequins. Some journalists and taste experts quickly debated if a beaded dress was appropriate for day wear.

The color of this lace itself was a very gentle, subtle tone of sage, but I called it "lemongrass" to express an emotion more than a color. I hoped this tone would evoke the idea of rebirth and renewal. This color expressed warmth and a pacific, calming emotion and symbolized a new day.

I have always loved colors that are difficult to describe, because that way, everyone can own them. To some, this

"lemongrass" color was more like a sunflower. It was later also described as pale gold, corn husk, mustard, sunshine, mellow yellow, sandy ochre and newborn celery. But that was the point: color and beauty are in the eye of the beholder, and therefore are open to many interpretations. The more something is multifaceted and can be interpreted in many different ways, the longer its lifespan and the wider its reach.

When I saw this cloth, I felt instantly that this was the one. I knew it could help make Michelle luminous. The light was going to emit from within. This historic moment had to have more than one dimension, and I knew I could create depth with this lace.

WITH THAT TINY LEMONGRASS LACE swatch, I had found my voice and was immediately inspired to start designing. Ruben immediately put in an order for the cloth at Forster Willi— and we instantly heard bad news. The company was closed for the Christmas holidays!

After a lot of back and forth pleading about how important this cloth was to me, and how much I really wanted to work with it, Ruben finally had to be honest and tell them what was happening: We might, or might not, be designing a dress for someone really, really important—

maybe, perhaps possibly, the next First Lady of the United States. This was really going out on a limb. After all, we still didn't know at that point whether Michelle would choose to wear my dress on Inauguration Day.

Ruben and I have always had very good relationships with our fabric suppliers. Textiles being so near and dear to my heart, we have always loved the fabric mills who make their cloth with love. As makers, it's easy to recognize when others have a love for what they do. It's evident in the work. Fortunately, the people at Forster Rohner were as excited as we were about the possibility of making a dress for Michelle Obama. They immediately reopened their workshop and worked feverishly to weave the luscious lemongrass wool lace. I ordered just what I needed and nothing more.

It was in the middle of December when I finally decided on this little bit of magical cloth. Most of my staff was getting ready to leave on Christmas vacation, and we were still eagerly waiting for the textile to arrive.

Finally, on a Saturday, we got word that the fabric had made it through a snowstorm on a flight and landed in New York City. Our Forster Willi contact in New York, Stuart, chased the delivery truck it was on all around town in the snow until he got the fabric and was able to hand-deliver the precious cargo to our studio.

Onto the cutting table Ruben and I leapt, working out the pattern pieces to make best use of the cloth. Ruben's dad, Vitelio, got busy cutting the many layers of inner lining that would complete the outfit. As one part was finished being cut, I would hand it off to one of my seamstresses. Little by little, the entire studio was put to work assembling the many parts as the coat and dress were lovingly, carefully assembled.

My studio worked feverishly to complete the ensemble. When it was finally and carefully packed away in a FedEx box, Ruben raced down the street just in the nick of time for next-day delivery. Off our ensemble went, with all of our best hopes and wishes. And off we went, for our winter vacation in Miami Beach to visit with my family over the Christmas holiday and into the New Year.

Life has a wonderful way of letting you forget where you just were, so that you can think only of the present. We had been so overwhelmed with work and deadlines through the rush of the maybe, possibly First Lady dress situation that we collapsed on the beach, exhausted but happy, and really rested and enjoyed the family time.

WE RETURNED TO NEW YORK on a frozen day in January and went right back to our overbooked schedule. There were many deadlines and projects we were dying to do—so many, in fact, that we forgot all about the dress.

Then, on January 20, the phone rang early in the morning. It was my mother-in-law, Oneida, asking if the dress that Mrs. Obama was wearing that morning was made by me. Ruben asked, "What does it look like?"

"It's made out of a very elaborate, intricate-looking fabric," she said. "It looks like it could be gold with embroidery."

"No, that doesn't sound like an Isabel dress," Ruben answered.

He assumed that Mrs. Obama had decided to wear someone else's design and hung up the phone, disappointed. He then darted downstairs to check his e-mail on the computer, which is how he starts every day. Ruben goes to his computer the way others pick up their morning papers at the front door.

Ruben nearly fell off his chair when he saw how many e-mails had already accumulated in his in-box. As he watched in astonishment, many more popped up. They were from *The New York Times*, *The Washington Post*, *The Financial Times*, and on and on, from newspapers all over the U.S., Japan, Italy, and other countries around the world. All of them asked the same questions: "Can you confirm? Is that an Isabel Toledo dress? Can you please confirm that Michelle Obama is wearing an Isabel Toledo dress?"

Ruben, of course, could not confirm any answer to the

journalists' questions. He dashed upstairs and turned on the television to see the dress for himself, but at that point the Obamas were inside the church. There was still no way to know.

Ruben ran back downstairs to get me and the seamstresses. We wouldn't all fit in the elevator, so some of us took the elevator and others ran up the stairs to gather around the television in the painting studio, collectively holding our breath until Michelle Obama emerged from the church.

When I saw her in my dress, it was like a gift from the universe. I was totally floating. Taken together, the lace and all of its secret layers created a wonderful effect. It was almost like little bits of sunshine were emanating from the dress and coat. I felt like my lemongrass dress and coat ensemble was happiness made visible—for Michelle and me, for our new president, and for a nation. That had been my prayer for that day, and it had been answered.

The response was instant and phenomenal. The entire world watched this gracious, humble, and modernly elegant woman step into the future and take us all along with her. Our computer eventually crashed from so many e-mails, and we had to stop answering the phone, as it was ringing nonstop.

I think that I absorbed the wave of energy that was felt by everybody at the same time, and that made the impact for us that much bigger. I was moved to tears, transported by the vision of Michelle and Barack Obama walking together. My staff and I stood together in front of the television in Ruben's studio in a giant circle. We were glued there for hours, until the very moment of the swearing-in ceremony. Then we suddenly all hugged and cried with joy!

To put this into perspective, you must remember that Ruben and I are both political refugees, and my staff consists of people from the U.S., China, Korea, Poland, Mexico, and Japan. We have interns from Austria, Qatar, England, and Canada. Ruben's eighty-five-year-old dad, who was our head cutter, had come from Cuba after the Revolution. So you can just imagine how proud and honored we all were, this small United Nations of Fashion. Watching this historic moment meant so much to us for all its deep significance. This was a moment bigger than fashion. This was history, and now we were woven into this very moment in history forever.

. . .

THAT FREEZING MONDAY MORNING, OUR studio on Broadway had reporters camped out in the lobby and spilling out into the street. The New York City police stopped by to check on us, just to make sure that there hadn't been a murder or some other tabloid-worthy incident. Alina Cho from CNN was the first reporter who managed to sneak up the fire stairs past the crowd and TV crews, who were not only from New York stations, but from France, Italy, Japan, Brazil, Germany, and Russia as well.

All of the shops that carry my collections, like Colette in Paris, Nordstrom in Seattle, and Septième Étage in Geneva, immediately experienced a run on their Toledo stock. Simon Doonan of Barneys had designed "Michelle Obama wears Isabel Toledo" windows by Tuesday morning.

The lemongrass lace ensemble has been called the most looked-at, most commented-on dress, and a dress seen by the most eyes at the same time ever. Partly this is because of the television and the Internet, but it is also because of the public's hunger for news about our new President and First Lady. The name "Isabel Toledo" on Google went from 45,000 listings to 200,000 listings in one day. We were certainly not prepared for the tidal wave of energy that came roaring toward us!

We are humbled to have played a part in this great moment in history. I feel sure that part of Michelle Obama's legacy, without sounding trivial, will include not only her great natural style, but her embrace of fashion design as part of the great American cultural dialogue, which keeps us at the forefront of developments. Mrs. Obama was not just wearing fashion on Inauguration Day. She was wearing culture.

THE BEAT GOES ON

Designing an outfit worn by the First Lady on Inauguration Day made the impossible possible: The name Isabel Toledo went from being an under-the-radar, well-kept secret to a global household name within twenty-four hours. I was declared the Patron Saint of Lace in Switzerland by the local papers, since this is where the lace had been made. A few more textile mills in Japan and Korea mistakenly claimed the same, all happy to be connected to this historic event.

We hadn't anticipated this rush of adrenaline and the happy chaos that followed Inauguration Day. What was most fascinating of all was to hear people tell me their stories when the dust finally settled. I loved hearing where they were and what they were doing on the morning of the inauguration. From cabdrivers to hairdressers, people continued to connect with me through that moment in time. The human quilt of experience continued to multiply. For me, this is precisely what fashion and culture are for: to communicate and connect.

THE EXHIBITION AT FIT OPENED a few months later and set attendance records at the museum. The lemongrass suit from Inauguration Day had a special place of honor, and was a magnet for audiences of designers and enthusiasts. It was a pleasure for me to see people of all ages, and from all walks of life, parading through the museum to see my work. The dialogue between art and fashion that Ruben and I had begun twenty-five years earlier was now being shared and absorbed by many people.

We had filled the space at FIT with as much information as possible. Now it was heartwarming to see fashion students sketching, architecture students discussing the connection between geometry and fashion design, and women telling stories about what they wore to get married or to go to their first day at work. The galleries were alive with sharing as the FIT exhibition generated a community experience, whether museumgoers were looking up at Ruben's mile-long watercolor scroll that documents my collections through the years, or studying the diagrams of my dress patterns displayed along with the clothes.

By showing others our personal road map, I hoped that we would somehow help jump-start and inspire the next generation of makers. It is sometimes difficult for people just starting out to figure out how to get there from here. There is no one road or doorway, and that's just the way it should be. All channels must be kept as open as possible to keep creativity flowing and the entrepreneurial spirit invigorated.

All of the interest shown during this exhibition allowed some interesting new business prospects to flourish. Some were hysterical, like the reality show offer that Ruben and I received, where the producer eagerly suggested that young fashion upstarts from different countries would be shipped to our studio. They would each work on a collection destined for their First Ladies' respective wardrobes! The thought that we would have to live with all of these people in our studio made us howl with laughter.

WEAVING TOGETHER HIGH AND LOW

Following the Obama inauguration, we agreed to enter into collaborations with two larger retail companies, Target and Payless ShoeSource. I was thrilled to be able to collaborate once again on designing fashion that can reach many people at once.

When you can combine what you love to do and help others while you're at it, this is bliss. The collaboration with Target began as part of a Harlem initiative; they were opening their first store in that neighborhood. One of Ruben's first questions when the Target executives proposed that we design resort wear for this big opening, was, "How many jobs will you be creating in the neighborhood?" The answer was, "Plenty."

Plus, Target was giving us the opportunity to donate five percent of our sales from that collection to El Museo del Barrio, a museum we had been involved with for the last five years, raising funds so that the museum could renovate and add a new wing. The museum means

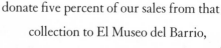

a lot to us because it was started by a local Puerto Rican teacher who wanted to show kids in the neighborhood the value of art in everyday life. El Museo has an "open art" policy that is inclusive, not exclusive. It is a museum that is very much about the local community, yet knows and speaks to the world with a specific Caribbean point of view.

For the Target collaboration, I was able to work with Ruben's artwork to create summer beach gear. I love to apply his drawings and images to my shapes. This merger always produces unexpected results. This time, I mixed his black ink calligraphy drawings for bikini bottoms with ultra-colorful insects flying across their mismatched bikini tops. Ruben's surreal landscape became my favorite pareo wrap. I sewed two together to make a caftan; three sewn together gave me a summer wrap dress.

Working on mass-produced projects like this gives me opportunities to push certain designs forward at a much more wallet-friendly price. For example, I was able to evolve my four-armhole dress into a T-shirt dress. The armholes are designed so that you can flip it over to form a cowl neckline and wear it as a tank top or a T-shirt dress. It was great to watch girls at Target examining that dress design. They would try it on and start to figure out the different ways they could wear it. To see the way that people style and come up with their own interpretations of my designs is always a learning experience for me.

I also revised the packing bag that I had originally created for Fiorucci in 1984 out of multicolored burlap. This time, I was able to take it to its logical conclusion in high-performance, quick-dry parachute nylon, with each panel a different color. It looked like a deflated beach ball until you put things inside, which made it expand into a giant globe. For Target, I added a netted mesh outer compartment to hold your flip-flops, sunglasses, and a magazine or two. This was yet more wonderful evidence that a great design has no expiration date.

The giant art beach towels we made were the first thing to sell out. Best of all, they were dedicated to El Museo, and featured a fanciful abstract portrait of me, complete with seashell hair. You can imagine my surprise when we recently spotted a woman on the street wearing her homemade version of a strapless summer dress with my face on her backside!

PAYLESS IN PARIS

I admire things that you can use on an everyday basis that are well designed and made with integrity, whether it's a spatula, a sewing machine, a jacket, a pair of carpenter's pants, or a pair of shoes. And, when I find something that I like to wear often, I buy it in multiples. Of course, to do this means that you need either a huge budget or affordable goodies.

I have a broad appreciation for shoes. In my early teens, I started a shoe collection. Some pairs were precious and rare, some were just basic, and some were just plain weird. In some cases, these gems were affordable and easy to find. One of my favorite styles was a pair of summer sandals I found at Woolworth's. The senior citizen crowd, who know a good thing when they see one, were very fond of these, too. These summer cotton sandals were just slightly wedged and came in basic black, cream, and red for spice. These Woolworth finds looked great with my short shorts, tube-legged Levi's, and just about anything else.

Before there was fashion, there was a great big world of merchandise. Some were hits and some were misses. But, if you had a good eye, you could really score and find treasures like those sandals that didn't cost much, but went far on style.

I became increasingly besotted with shoes the older I got. When I started going to dance clubs, my footwear became even more important. Dance steps look best in a great pair of shoes, whether they're thin-soled, high-heeled naked sandals with crisscrossed straps up the leg, or platform sandals with Roman lacework that make you feel towering on the dance floor.

And, as Mrs. Vreeland witnessed when I was her intern at the Met, no shoes are too big or too small for me: if I love them, I will find a way to wear them, even if it means layering my slippers into a pair of men's sandals. Ruben laughs and says that, if someone broke into my shoe closet, they would not have a clue who could wear such a variety of footwear. My shoe taste casts a very wide scope, and I really do wear them all. I can walk for miles around New York City in what seem to be improbably tall heels, since my husband and I both love to walk. The very next day, though, I might feature a pair of my sensible librarian shoes that I collect by the dozen when I can find them.

As Marilyn Monroe once said, "Give a girl the right shoes, and she can conquer the world." Marilyn and my mom, Berthy, were of the same opinion when it came to shoes. But the key word here is "right." Right for whom, and for what? Shoes are as personal and complex as women themselves. For some, a pair of high heels and shorts with a sweater is their daily bread. For other women, nothing but high-top sneakers in every color is what they require. More power to you, I say. As long as you can make them work, that's the only rule to follow.

I have always dressed from the bottom up. By this, I mean that I start with my shoes. I let my feet do the talking and let them set the pace for the day. Once my feet have expressed themselves, the rest of my outfit flows from there. Shoes can dictate your body language and your posture, which is why I start dressing at the feet.

It's easy to see, then, why I was so delighted to collaborate with Payless, where I now have the golden opportunity to work on shoe designs that are produced for all women everywhere. I love knowing that I am designing a great product with smart lines, a product that is well made and will be sold at an affordable price. Because I love finding inexpensive design treasures with unique and memorable details, I hope that I am supplying the same kind of treasures for another generation of women. It is a wonderful validation to see my work magnified into this whole other stratosphere.

My collaboration with Payless has resulted in strong and bold modern shapes that are easily identifiable by the Isabel Toledo fingerprint in the details. I love the juxtaposition of materials and textures combined in an elegant gesture. Your feet should always look distinctive while feeling at ease. I am very big on the comfort level; if a pair of shoes isn't comfortable, it doesn't make it to the sales floor.

I like designs that can be produced in a million different colors. This way, women can retain their individuality while still having access to a well-made mass-produced beauty. I love this aspect of mass production— its ability to supply a super well-made design. Basic enough to work for many but individual enough to be distinctive. I love spotting a stylish woman in any part of the world wearing a pair of Isabel Toledo for Payless Shoes.

The icing on the cake was seeing them in Paris. For some reason, Payless in Paris has a very satisfying ring to it. I did premiere the collection at Colette on the Rue St.-Honoré. To see women with Goyard bags snapping up two or three pairs at a time was a personal pleasure. I love how good design transcends language and even style. Good designs find its way into your wardrobe and end up being one of the favorite things that you pick up again and again. This durability and user-friendly aspect is what I most adore. This is what makes an item become a must-have.

This feeling of finding a treasure is what I remember about my early teen Woolworth finds.

GLASS HOUSE

The opportunity to share and give back to the culture of art and creativity is always a mental workout. Sometimes, it can also be a physical one, as Ruben and I discovered recently when we had the honor to be artists-in-residence at the Pilchuck Glass School, founded by Dale Chihuly, for part of one lovely hot summer.

We had this opportunity because our friends at Nordstrom had hosted a fashion show for me at Dale Chihuly's boathouse studio about five years earlier. To see the models wearing my clothes and parading in front of boiling-hot furnaces was unforgettable. While the models drifted in and out of sight in their chiffon and liquid jersey dresses, the glassblowers

carried out their highly choreographed dance. A crew of four
or five of them, all tightly moving together like a dance troupe,
manipulated hot liquid glass in front of the furnace. After that
spectacular introduction to the magic world of glass, Ruben
and I jumped at the opportunity to serve as artists-in-residence
at the Pilchuck Glass School.

Believe it or not, the biggest drawback was time. Since
we run our own business on four floors of a midtown studio,
being away for that amount of time isn't easy. That is the big
downside of rowing your own boat: You can't really put down
the oars, or you stop moving. Luckily, I was able to arrange my
production and shipment of collections to give my staff time
off, too. With a bag packed full of carpenter's pants, sweaters,
and raincoats, off we went into the mountains near Seattle.

We were immediately awed by the setting: a vast wonderland of pine forests, deer, hawks, and horses that we soon encountered. The Pilchuck School is nestled inside a forest, and you start each day by being awakened at seven forty-five by a jangling cowbell calling us all in for hot coffee, eggs, toast, and whatever other delicious things they might be inspired to cook for you. The food was as fresh and outdoorsy as you can imagine, and served in the lodge on giant, long cedar tables.

After breakfast, everyone went off to take their classes with master teachers. Ruben and I had adjoining studio cabins; we worked together, as usual, in one cabin, and used the other to house our experiments in "glass gone wrong." This eventually became known as "The Toledo graveyard," where glass ideas went to rest until we needed to bring them back for inspiration.

We deliberately did not research glassblowing or think about it too much ahead of time, because we wanted to see what would happen organically, with no preconceived ideas. When we arrived, we first observed the master blowers and the students at work, so that we could try to absorb all of the different ways that glass is handled and manipulated.

During our stay, Ruben and I collaborated with just about every glass department available at Pilchuck. From blowing glass to casting it, etching it, and painting on it, the possibilities are endless. Our cabin soon became a wall-to-wall reference library of glass ideas. Ruben's watercolor sketches filled the available wall space from floor to ceiling.

We left our windows and doors open constantly, so that both students and master teachers could drop in and take whatever ideas they wanted to use as inspiration. This was our open-door collaboration project. It was a treat to see how different people interpreted our lines and forms; they were all related, but not the same. Originality is really in the hands of the artist. Even when two of you are making the same thing, it will come out differently.

All this artistic madness never stopped, unless it was for lunch at noon or dinner at six. After dinner, some students even headed back to the classrooms for late-night creative powwows. Most of the action hovered around the open-air glassblowing studio with its ultra-hot furnaces; because of the heat, glassblowing was best done outdoors and in the cool night air.

Ruben and I were captivated by these glassblowing lessons.

Ruben was so entranced that he created a series of ink drawings depicting the different movements and gestures of this complex choreography. In his drawings, you can see the intensity and control, the unspoken communication between the glass team required to blow these sometimes huge but delicate vessels.

He was able to capture this right from the core. I had set up Ruben's drawing table right in the middle of this hot, smoky pit. He got to work only after we had gotten to know the glassblowers well enough to gain their confidence, and vice versa; glassblowing requires trust in your partners, since you're all handling burning-hot cannonballs of liquid glass able to melt the skin off your bones.

Ruben beautifully captured this strange dance, which looks like a cross between a bullfight and a ballet. It is elegant, yet dangerous because of the roaring fires all around. At night, this outdoor fire arena resembles a nightclub at the mouth of a volcano, especially because great music is blasting away while everyone is deeply involved in making glass.

One of our favorite things to do was to walk off into the dark hills and look down upon this glowing scene, while the clear night sky was assaulted by meteor showers so graphic, they resembled animated cartoons. If we happened to wake up in the middle of the night, we couldn't help but take a look outside from our balcony. We always watched the sky for these special effects, and one night we were well rewarded by the dazzling, mystical light show of the Aurora Borealis.

Ruben and I came home from our retreat with a giant perfume bottle made by glass master Roger Parramore from one of Ruben's designs. The bottle looks as if it has a face and chandelier earrings, and its gangly handles resemble hands resting on hips. It is a striking interpretation of a watercolor drawing. The way Roger "paints" with the subtleties of colored glass are remarkably close to Ruben's painting. Roger's glass shapes seem to make living gestures, like the movements of a paintbrush.

I was also thrilled to collaborate with Preston Singletary on several glass forms that abstractly mimic some of my dress shapes. Preston expertly etched the glass forms with tattoolike shapes based on my dress patterns. The almost tribal appearance of the patterns etched into the vessels has a Native American presence, very much in keeping with Preston's brilliant body of work, which is full of the ancient magic of the Pacific Northwest.

Fashion and glass, I discovered, have a surprising amount in common. While watching how blowers work hot glass, I was struck by how similar the process was to the way I work directly with cloth: We do things quickly and instinctively, letting gravity do a lot of the work. Glass takes on its own momentum, like fabric, and the masters learn how to manipulate it and let it do its wondrous thing, all the while making new and surprising forms, adding their particular strokes of genius to whatever nature is already doing. It was an honor to once again be part of an artistic collaboration that stretched my thinking as a designer and artist.

DR. TOLEDO X 2

Working with design students has always been a priority for Ruben and me. We both learned to swim our way through the creative waters of New York City by following our instincts at every stage of our life and work. Now we're eager to share what we've learned.

In addition to the joy I find in working with students, I also find great pleasure in working closely with their teachers. The professors are the ones responsible, season after season, year after year, for continuing to help grow good crops of students. Otis College of Art and Design is a great example of this. I have worked with Otis for over ten years, ever since fashion designer Rosemary Brantley, the founding chair of that college's Fashion Department, called on us to do a senior design project with some of her students. Our friend Todd Oldham had recommended Ruben and me, because Todd had experienced the Toledo cross-pollination of fashion and art ideas firsthand many times. He knew that we enjoyed collaborating with others on creative endeavors, big and small.

It's fascinating to see the different ways that design students think and work. They bring varied experiences and learning styles to the sketchpad, cutting table, and sewing machine. Some students learn best by observing closely, some through doing things by themselves, and others through experimentation. Some students are hard to crack, while others are immediately open to new ideas. We all think and work differently, and this is essential for cultural diversity. To be able to arrive at your own unique vision by following your particular road is a blessing not only for students and designers, but for the rest of the world, too.

The best atmosphere for learning has the same qualities as a great environment for working. There has to be an open dialogue, where anything and everything is possible, but where technique, craft, and perfection are not dirty words. Once design students learn to value making things with their hands,

they can achieve anything their minds dream up. To make something yourself is a very powerful act. Ruben likes to tell them, "Just because you can draw, that doesn't mean you can make."

This is a good case for the love of craft. To make something with your own hands is something entirely different from sketching out an idea. This is valuable, too, but when you actually, physically make something yourself, nobody can stop you from completing your thoughts and accomplishing something.

Ruben and I like working with classes together, because we enjoy the collaborative teaching-mentoring method. Since no two people think alike, it is healthy for students to be exposed to more than one idea at a time. They have to process a few different angles and opinions all at once. This fragmented thinking process is much like real life, especially in matters of art or fashion, where there is no specific right or wrong answer but a series of trial-and-error propositions to conquer.

When Otis College of Art and Design's President Samuel Hoi presented us with honorary doctorates in the fine arts, Ruben and I became Dr. Toledo times two. This honor came with a new sense of responsibility for me, because it raised

the bar on how much we have benefited by the largesse
of this American way of life. This honorary doctorate is a
corroboration of the fulfillment of the real possibilities of the
American dream. This is an endless dream, dreamed by many
and in as many different tongues—the freedom to not be
blocked from dreaming and achieving. Billie Holiday once said
that America produces raw talent and allows it to reach the
top. That is the real American dream turned into reality.

The American dream is a lifestyle and a state of mind. It is
a sensibility that I add into the clothes that I design. It is the
freedom to dream, imagine whatever you want to be, and the
perseverance to achieve it stitch by stitch. More than anything
else, I want to be sure that my industry continues to grow and
evolve, so that it can express and reflect the rich social texture
of this country.

There is no road map or safety net when you're an artist.
Sometimes you feel very sure of your direction. Sometimes,
it's a complete surprise. Art is about discovery, invention, and
embracing every opportunity to learn something new that
comes your way.

R. Toledo

conclusion

Conclusion

TRUE TO MY CHARACTER, I HAVE
found that life needs to repeat itself to
have the most satisfying meaning. Some
of the patterns that arise have become my
body of work.

As this book goes to print, Ruben and I are preparing for an exhibition event in Miami's Freedom Tower Museum. We have come full circle, as this is our Ellis Island, the very place that most Cuban refugees entered the United States. Sacred ground? Almost. It is certainly emotional and living proof of the wonderful motion of life's patterns.

My parents aren't here to see our exhibition in the flesh. But they are certainly with us in spirit, as are all of the people in my hometown of Camajuani who lent their spirit of inspiration to my work and to this story. This is how I entered my life and my book, and how I will leave you now, dear reader. But before we say good-bye, I'd like to pass on a few fashion acupuncture points, which are what I like to call those tried-and-tested observations that have worked so well for me. Feel free to add your own.

- ➤ Keep your mystery. Value your style secrets as you would your family jewels. This is your personality.
- ➤ Try dressing from the bottom up: I let my shoes set the mood. This gives me the sense of proportion and helps inform my body language for the day. Get to know and feel who you are in platforms, sneakers, stiletto heels or sensible walking shoes. By aligning your mood to your shoes, you amplify your ability to communicate.
- ➤ Pockets are your best friends. I insist on having pockets in most things I make and wear for practical reasons. I also find pockets help give a woman body language and a certain authority. That said, as I grow older, I find that knowing how to use your hands is an art in itself. This is what separates the woman from the girls.
- ➤ Don't be afraid to be appropriate. It has become a dirty word in fashion and style talk. But for me, being appropriate means simply being in touch with the

moment. When you are in touch with the moment, with yourself, you communicate effortlessly.

- In fashion, all the wrongs are one day so right.

- An organized closet provides a bird's-eye view of who you are. I organize my closet by category. This is an easy-to-spot formula—a section for pants, another for skirts, jackets, shirts or blouses, and another section of dresses. With time, you can easily read the language of your own wardrobe. Your eyes will quickly spot the color or the texture or the silhouette that your unconscious fashion instinct is requesting. Always follow your instinct.

- I am organized, because I am lazy. One of my lazy dressing tricks is to have in my formal wardrobe a few garments I call my background dressing items. This is usually a black, perfectly chic and practical outfit that I can wear when I do not want to be in bloom. This mini chic wardrobe must be as dependable as a tuxedo is in a man's wardrobe.

- My personal favorite habit and exercise is breathing. Breathe deeply as often as you remember to. Your stomach really gets a workout.

- Keep your core strong and healthy. Try wearing a belt to remind you to stand straight, and avoid carrying too heavy a shoulder bag on the same shoulder. This will throw you off balance and tilt your shoulder.

- The best kind of advice to get is the one you steal. Don't ever pass up any advice overheard or given to someone else. It's guilt-free.
- The only way to create luxury is to love your craft and the way to create fashion is through the love of innovation. Innovation applied to fine craftsmanship equals high fashion.
- A well-woven society cultivates a free flow of culture. This enriches us all.
- When we are young, we are formed. As we grow older, we are informed.
- To make up or make down is a woman's personal expression as an artist. I find the more lines on my face, the less makeup I apply. When applying lipstick, I consider whether I wish to impose upon or blend in with my surroundings. I either dab it on for a fresh light touch or I paint my lips to define my mood. This allows me to achieve a different mood from the same lipstick color.
- I like to shop when I travel. It becomes more of a cultural experience.
- Packing can be seen as an art or a science. As a child, I watched my mother pack, and for her it was all

or nothing. She simply started packing way before her departure date and employed the art of folding until she had packed practically everything in her wardrobe. Carry-on generation—when it came time for me to pack, I turned it into a science. Pick luggage to suit your scale. The length of your suitcase should fit your clothes with only one fold. Pants folded in half, at your knee, your dresses folded at the waist. Jackets travel best inside out, sleeves left tucked inside. Your socks fill in the corners of a suitcase and keep it all from collapsing.

➡ Mind travel—learn to roughly picture the days you will be traveling and dress them in your mind's eye, then divide them in half. Half of those days are your ideal looks; the other half will be a combination of the outfits. Dresses can be layered with sweaters for a change. Consider wearing your longest, bulkiest items instead of packing them. Shoes should be versatile. For evening, metallics work with all colors; they have no specific season connotation. I travel in stylish walking shoes and negotiate another pair depending on the space left in the suitcase.

➡ When designing, I don't aim for contemporary. I love the timeless; this becomes contemporary when needed.

- As a young girl, one of the most astonishing things I observed in the women around me was the many different ways they communicated. Some said it all with their eyes, others mesmerized with the sound of their voice, while others used their hands and arms as magic wands. Learn to use all your gifts to elevate and communicate.

- Learn to love your ugly ducklings. Your creative mistakes contain the seeds of your future successes, so do not discard them.

- My fashion mantra, if I have one at all, is amuse and confuse, relax and enjoy. I am all about freedom of expression. I reserve the liberty and freedom to change my mind and clothes as often as I can.

The End

My sincerest, full-hearted THANK YOU to Holly Robinson, for helping me put my words and stories into this beautiful book format, and to Sandra Guzman, Tracy Bernstein, Kim Suarez, and Ray Garcia (the patient instigator publisher) and the whole ghost town of writers who helped quilt this book together. Thank you to Pauline for her caring eye.

FOREVER RUBEN who is the warmest part of me I have no control over.

A special thanks to Margaret Hayes, President of Fashion Group, for establishing the FGI–Isabel and Ruben Toledo Endowed Scholarship Fund in 2006 at The Fashion Institute of Technology in New York City.